A RANSOM
FOR
WURMBRAND

A RANSOM FOR WURMBRAND

by

ANUTZA MOISE

Edited by
Myrtle Powley

ZONDERVAN PUBLISHING HOUSE
A DIVISION OF THE ZONDERVAN CORPORATION
GRAND RAPIDS, MICHIGAN

A Ransom for Wurmbrand
Published in the United Kingdom as
One of God's Smallest
Copyright © 1972 by Anutza Moise

Second printing September 1972

Library of Congress Catalog Card Number 72-83869

Published by special arrangement with
Hodder and Stoughton Limited.

Printed in the United States of America

Contents

48588

Prologue

WHEN, IN THE SUMMER of 1964, I received the news that Richard Wurmbrand had been released from prison, I burst into tears of joy. At last, after so many years, my prayers and those of countless others had been answered.

Richard and his wife Sabina, known to all as Bintzea, were and are my closest friends on earth. At that time I had not seen them for seventeen years, not since, myself a refugee from communism, I had said goodbye to them in Bucharest and made my way illegally over the frontier in a nightmare journey to the West and freedom. I had tried hard then to persuade them to come with me. But they had refused, feeling that God still had a work for them to do in Rumania.

Since then they had been through unspeakable hardships. Both had been in prison and labour camps, Richard for a total of fourteen years. Something of how that experience had marked him was revealed in a strange and remarkable letter he wrote to me a few weeks after his release. I was to learn more later, when we met in the West. For Richard's release from prison was only the first step towards the objective for which I had been working and praying for so long — that of bringing Richard and Bintzea and their son Mihai to the free world.

Our dear Anutza [Richard wrote],

We have received your letter. It has also been brought to our knowledge that we have got the visa. For the moment we have no more idea than you when or if we are coming.

I am slowly getting used again to my new circumstances of life. I am finding, too, that one's spiritual life takes on new aspects when one is back in family life.

Separated from my family and from the brethren, I was conscious that I was enfolded in divine embraces. But they were like a cloud embracing the snow-covered mountain peaks. That companionship with God was like a frozen lake which reflects the cold bright light of the moon. In that embrace — as in a fire that is slowly extinguished — every personal desire died; or, better still, fell asleep on the breast of the Saviour; because each separate desire of the self is like the adulterous act of a queen. There is no sense in asking the Saviour even once: "Do you want me to do this, or that?" What He wants has been revealed and inscribed from all eternity in our new being. Quietly, without even asking a single question, I simply rested.

Now such a thing is no longer possible. Life has once again caught me up in its storm. I am dizzy with so many impressions, problems, new duties. How complicated everything is in your world, and how simple it was in the world from which I have come! In your world, your every action catches you up in an immense cog wheel with no visible ending. Nobody can commit *one* sin, because this one sin releases and involves thousands of others. You cannot strike a guilty person without causing others who are not guilty to suffer on account of it. For instance, you send a thief to prison, but as a consequence his innocent young children will suffer. In the world below, every gesture, every action, can release great tragedies at an immense distance.

There was a man in Bethlehem who did a good deed: he gave shelter to the Lord's mother so that she should bear Him in a stable. The dramatic consequence was that all the babies in that town had to die. In the world below, no action can be calculated. You cannot know the consequences of your deeds — even the good ones; while in the world of the spirit, which I have been inhabiting up to the present, without the possibility of exteriorising, murders did not murder, thefts did not dispossess, lies did not deceive. Everything that happened took place only in my inner self. And the beauties and joys were always pure.

Now I no longer have this privilege. Sin watches over every step you make, even when you are doing good, even when you are fulfilling God's law. Here you can live only through grace, only by trusting God's compassion and wisdom, which will solve all problems. That is why I agree with Luther when he says that "the Law is a word of perdition, of wrath, of sadness, a word of pain. The Law is the word of the Judge to the accused, a word of disturbance and of cursing." The Law of God gives us a guilty conscience, an unquiet heart, a heart that trembles because of the sins which the Law discloses to us without being able to remove them from us. Without it, we live in quiet trust that God is guiding our steps through the maze of our lives — even when things happen to us or we are doing things which we ourselves do not understand.

Give our love to all our dear ones. In a few days I shall be going to a sanatorium at the seaside. Perhaps Bintzea will come too, to stay near me for a few days. In my opinion she needs a rest more than I do.

I embrace you.
RICHARD

As it happened, more than a year was to pass before I welcomed them, late one freezing December night, at the air terminal at Oslo. I was overjoyed to see them. We were none of us the same people we had been. But our friendship had remained unchanged.

Life is full of new beginnings. We were now all three over

fifty, at an age when most people expect to have settled into some sort of security. Richard and Bintzea were destitute, having had to leave behind what few possessions they had. As for me, a constant battle with arthritis had forced me to give up my job, and I had little hope of finding another. A few months ago, it had looked as if my active days might be over. I was soon going to find myself busier than I had ever been.

Richard had emerged from the fires of suffering with a deep awareness of the reality of God, and of the spiritual realms where the powers of good and evil do battle for men's souls. He had seen communism as a stronghold of these evil powers and resolved to devote all his energies to winning the communist world for Christ.

It has been my great privilege to be associated with Richard's work since he has been in the West. More than anyone else in the past few years, he has been the means of awakening complacent Christians to the evils of the anti-God totalitarian system which rules over so great a part of the world, and to the sufferings of those who try to bear witness for Christ within that system. He has founded Missions to the Communist World in twenty-seven different countries. Through his preaching and his books he has raised money which has been used to help those who are suffering for their faith, and I have been able to play a part in getting this help to those who need it.

Had anyone told me, when I was a girl in Rumania, of the turn my life was to take, I would have found it difficult to believe them. But looking back, it seems that in a way all my life has been a preparation for this task.

I

Childhood

I WAS TWO AND a half when my mother died. The day of her funeral is my earliest distinct memory. I can still recall quite clearly the sense of desolation and bewilderment; how I cried, and ran after the men who were carrying her out, and how my grandmother took me in her arms and comforted me. It was July 1916.

My father was not at home at that time. As a matter of fact, he had not yet seen me. He had left for Canada in November 1913 before I was born, and because my mother was pregnant they had decided that she would follow him with the children as soon as she was able. But World War I broke out, and my father never saw my mother again.

With my brother, Haim, and my sister, Rachel, I continued to live in my grandmother's home. As she owned a small restaurant, we never went hungry in spite of war-time shortages. We children were very much spoiled by the rest of the family, particularly by my Aunt Fanny and my Uncle Milo. Uncle Milo was so young that I looked on him as an older playmate. He used to chase me round the table and toss me in the air, and was always thinking up new ways to amuse me. As for Aunt Fanny, I thought she was the most beautiful person in the world, and I loved her dearly. She must have had a prophetic insight — she suddenly started calling me *Yeshulein*, which is Yiddish for 'little Jesus'.

In spite of being thoroughly spoiled, I missed having a mother and father like other children. It seemed to me that some of the children I knew did not love their parents at all, and I could not understand it. "If I had a mother and father, I should love them so much," I used to say to Grandmother. However, my mother was dead, and I didn't know where my father was.

But in 1919 he returned. My grandmother, who was very fat, was in the lavatory in the courtyard when she heard a sudden commotion of people running and shouting. As she was wondering what all the fuss was about, someone banged on the door and called out, "Aunt Esther, Aunt Esther, Yitzik has come home!" Grandmother fainted with shock and fell to the floor, which gave way under her weight. They had some difficulty in getting her out and carrying her back into the house.

To add to the general confusion, two men had started a fight in the pub on the corner of our street, and the police had been called. It seemed that the entire neighbourhood was running to our house to welcome my father, while further down the street the police were trying to restore order and crowds of curious passers-by stopped to see what was going on. The whole street was like an overturned beehive.

Inside our house, however, there was a joyful reunion, tempered with sorrow that my mother had not lived to see my father again. I, who had longed so much for my father's return, did not dare to go near this strange, handsome man. It was days before I found my way to his lap of my own accord, but from that time on we were great friends until he died in 1946.

We continued to live with my mother's family until the following year when they all decided to emigrate to America. Grandmother tried hard to persuade my father to join them, but he preferred to stay in Rumania. He would not even hear of her suggestion that he should let her take Rachel, Haim and me. Like all Jewish parents, he loved his children dearly. So in the end they went without us, and we stayed on in the house, a little family without a mother.

Conditions were very hard all over Europe in those post-war years, and Rumania was no exception; there was a great deal of unemployment and desperate poverty. My father was lucky enough to get a job with the Red Cross, in charge of relief work. This meant that we had to move to Constanza, where we actually lived in the palace where the King and Queen used to stay when they visited this Black Sea resort. They had graciously put it at the disposal of the relief work. I remember most of all the lovely big park full of flowers and butterflies, where I liked to play. We had a governess to look after us, and I felt like a real princess.

However, after a couple of years the Red Cross closed down its work, and my father found himself out of a job. We were now in for a really difficult time. We moved to Daddy's native village, where his only sister was still living. This aunt was married to a baker, and they had a large family. At first we were able to live on the money Daddy had earned in Constanza; he rented a house and paid a woman to take care of us. When the money had run out and he still had no work, he asked Aunt Sofi to let us live with her.

I was very fond of my aunt, but her husband, who was rather mean about money, did not at all relish the idea of having another three mouths to feed. Our cousins were like most children — when they had been up to something they said that we had done it. Two of them in particular took delight in pinching us whenever the grown-ups were not looking; and I was constantly covered in bruises. Haim, Rachel and I did better than our cousins at school, and this was another matter for trouble between us. Whenever they could play a trick on us, they made the most of the opportunity. Fortunately, Aunt Sofi and the two eldest children understood what was going on, and took our side against the younger ones. So the time spent in my aunt's home was not altogether unhappy.

It was at this time that I first began to experience a deep

longing for God. I remember going to synagogue every Saturday with the whole family and coming home to a good dinner — then the quiet of the afternoon while the grown-ups were having a nap, and I would sit looking out of the window, trying to find God somewhere, yet feeling that He was so far away.

This very real hunger for God increased with every Sabbath day, but there was nobody with whom I could discuss my problem. So I tried to be good and obedient, so that I should at least please God in this respect. When I was out walking, I was always careful to cross the street when I came to a church, as I had been taught, so that I was not polluted by passing it too closely. If I came across a picture of Jesus in a school book, I would cover it with my hand when I had to turn the page, lest I should sin by looking at it.

The day came when my uncle tired of us, and packed our suitcases and took us off to find my father. We had a wait of several hours at Ploesti where we changed trains. A man who took a fancy to me gave me some money, which my uncle promptly took from me and went off to buy himself a drink. Once in the pub he forgot all about us, and when he at length returned, our train had left long ago. We had to sit on the station all night before another train arrived.

When at last we got to our destination, Daddy was not there, and nobody could tell us where he had gone. So there was nothing for my uncle to do but to take us back. Our cousins started a fresh campaign of teasing and pinching us, so that the bruises on our hearts were even greater than those that could be seen. When Daddy returned to his lodgings and heard what had happened, he came to fetch us away.

I was by this time seven and a half years old.

For a widower with three children, who had to go out to work with nobody to leave in charge of them, life was something of a problem. Then one of Daddy's friends told him about a school run by foreign teachers who took in boarders, and he suggested there might be a place for us.

So one bitterly cold February day in 1922 Daddy told us, "Get your coats on. We're going for a walk."

"Where are we going?" I wanted to know.

"Wait and see," was all he would say.

We set out to walk to the other side of the town. It seemed as though we were walking for hours. Every time I asked where we were going, I got the same answer: "Wait and see."

At last we turned in through a squeaky gate into a wide courtyard where a large, wolf-like dog started to bark his heart out at the sight of us. This animal was later to become a good friend of mine, but at that moment it was good to have my father's hand to take hold of.

Inside the house we were greeted by two ladies, one young and pretty, the other middle-aged and severe. I thought the younger one looked like pictures I had seen of angels. Only the wings were missing. She radiated a peace and gentleness I had never experienced before, and intuitively my heart went out to her. This was Olga Olaussen, who some years before had devoted her life to the service of the Norwegian Mission to the Jews, the *Israelsmisjonen*. She was so kind that when the time came for Daddy to leave us, and I understood that we were to remain behind, I was not as sorry as I might have been to be left among strangers. My spirit had already been touched by the love and peace which had enveloped me from the moment I had entered the house.

The *Israelsmisjonen* ran a school for girls in Galatz, of which the principal was Miss Antonia Aniksdal, whom we called Herzi because she was so *herzig*, the German word for sweet. Rachel was sent to this school, and Haim also went to a school in the town, but as I was considered rather delicate and undersized for my age, I was given lessons at home. Daddy had promised to come and visit us every Sunday, so I was quite happy — we had regular meals, a clean house and everything we children needed — though at first I missed him very much.

On the first Saturday after our arrival we were told we were to attend something which they called Sabbath School. This was really Sunday School, but it took place on Saturday afternoons.

The hall was full of children, and this was the first time I saw Herzi. After we had sung some hymns, she began to tell us a story. It was about a poor widow who had lost her only son, and now on the way to the cemetery she was weeping bitterly. I was soon sobbing heartily too, remembering my mother's funeral and how terrible it was to lose somebody you loved.

Still crying, I listened with particular attention to what Herzi was saying. She told us how a man called Jesus had met the funeral procession, and how, when He saw the woman weeping, He stopped and comforted her. Then He spoke to the boy who was dead, and the boy sat up and was dead no longer.

I was normally a very shy child, but I was so struck by this wonderful story that I jumped to my feet and asked loudly, "Is it true?"

Herzi answered, "Yes, it is quite true."

I had to be sure, so I asked again, "Is it really true?"

Herzi replied, gravely, "Really true."

I clapped my hands together and laughed for joy, and the joy I felt then has pervaded all my life ever since. Though I had never known about Him before, from that moment I believed in Jesus. And this I consider as my conversion.

Later, when I grew older and encountered the hardships of life, I had to fight many a battle to keep my faith, but the Lord Jesus Christ has always proved to be true. My longing and hunger for God were satisfied by Him that afternoon when I was still only a child.

2

New Friends

WINTER PASSED, AND WITH the coming of spring the Mission was invaded by young *halutzim*, pioneers who came mostly from Poland on their way to make a new home in Palestine. While they were waiting for their papers to come through they stayed with us, and so had an opportunity to hear the Gospel. Many contacts were made here, and the Mission resounded to the joyous singing of the young people. They sang mostly Hebrew patriotic songs, but they also learned some Christian hymns. I envied them for going to the country where Jesus had lived.

In the summer we went to the mountains, and for me this meant more than the fresh air. I made two very dear friends in Vulcan in Transylvania. One was a very old lady. Martha Galka had been a schoolteacher, but was now retired and living with her two sisters in a little house on the edge of the wood. I have rarely seen a woman who was so ugly to look at, but Martha had an inner radiance so great that when you looked at her you saw only this radiance.

A truly beautiful friendship bound together this old woman and the little eight-year-old girl. She told me about Jesus and all kinds of wonderful things, and my heart was like a garden, absorbing all the sunshine it had missed for so long, so that the flower of the love of God through Jesus Christ could spring out into full blossom.

One summer on our arrival at Vulcan we were met with the news that she had died some days previously, but we had come just in time for her funeral. I wept buckets of tears at the thought that I would not see her again on earth. It was the second time that death had taken away someone I loved, but this time I was comforted by the thought that Jesus would raise us from the dead.

An even stranger friendship was formed that first summer. The village was famous for the purity of its air, and for this reason a young Bessarabian man — let us call him Ivan — used to spend every summer there, as he suffered from tuberculosis. Ivan was about thirty, and unmarried. He took me for walks in the woods, taught me choruses and Bible verses, and we became inseparable. Soon he began calling me *ficutza*, which means 'little daughter' in Rumanian, and I called him *Papotchka*, Russian for 'little father'.

Many years later, I was to see a French film, *Sundays with Cybelle*, which vividly brought back to me our friendship. In the film the friendship between the little girl and the American soldier had a tragic ending, as did mine with Papotchka. When the Russians took Bessarabia from Rumania in 1939, Ivan was one of the first Christians to be deported to Siberia. There he was subjected to torture, and some years later he died. Fortunately neither of us knew in those early, happy days, what life had in store for us.

So the summers in Vulcan were sunny in more ways than one. When the autumn came and we had to part, we wrote each other long letters. One summer Ivan appeared with a young woman, whom he introduced as his wife. She was a tiny thing with blue eyes and a lovely smile. One might have thought that the little girl and the young wife would be jealous of each other — the child because she had to share Papotchka's love and friendship, and the young wife because her husband did not give her all his attention during their honeymoon. But the strange thing was that we two also became great friends. And years later, when we did not know what had happened to Ivan after he had been deported and she had moved to Bucharest, I was able to comfort Fedora and tried in every way possible to be of help to her.

In the autumn, when we returned to Galatz, the Mission was once again invaded by the *halutzim*. Then winter came, and with it my first Christmas. Something mysterious had been going on for days. We children, who had never had a Christian Christmas, wondered what it was all about.

One afternoon we were dressed up in fancy costumes, and taken to another building in the Mission, where all the *halutzim* were waiting for us. A little boy kept saying, "I want to see the candles, I want to see the candles." What candles? I wondered.

We sat down at a long table, and after a bountiful dinner the doors to the sitting-room were flung open and there, in the middle of the room, stood an enormous tree, decorated with beautiful toys and pictures, and lit by innumerable candles. Oh, the wonder of it! Never in my life had I beheld such a tree! So this was what the little boy had wanted to see. No wonder he was so excited.

Under the tree were piled heaps of parcels wrapped in coloured paper. Herzi read the Christmas Gospel, we sang carols, and at last the time came to distribute the parcels. I was dressed as an angel and went round to everybody with their presents. The joy and surprise at receiving gifts was visible in every face. It was so unexpected.

Hardly anybody present, apart from the missionaries, knew what Christmas was — the *halutzim* from Poland, especially, had experienced something quite different when the Christian festivals were celebrated. Those days had been set aside for Jew-beatings and pogroms. Though I had not had such sad experiences, neither had I ever shared in such great joy. And to crown this wonderful evening, I received my own most precious gift, a New Testament, with the promise of a whole Bible if I had finished reading it by next Christmas. So when the next Christmas came round I received my very first Bible.

The main work of the *Israelsmisjonen,* which had at that time no men on the staff, was among women and children. So I found another friend. Lina Poliakoff was the niece of the first convert in Galatz, Aunt Dora as we called her. Aunt Dora was my teacher, and now she became Lina's also. Lina was from Bessarabia, so she was probably deported or killed when the Germans invaded in 1940. We never heard from her or her family, or from many others of our Jewish and Hebrew Christian friends after that.

As time went on, many other girls and some boys were brought up by the Mission, so that we became a large family. Sister Olga was in charge of all practical matters, and was like a mother to us.

Rachel and Haim left the Mission after a few years and went to live with my father. I often went to visit them, or Daddy would come to see me. Sundays were days to look forward to. He used to take us out for walks, and I was always favoured with one of his hands. The other two had to share the second hand. I still remember the feel of his warm fingers clasping mine. He loved us dearly, and we loved him in return. The only thing which saddened him was that I used to talk abut Jesus.

My favourite walk on Sundays was to a public park, where there were a great many beautiful flowers, especially pansies, which I liked best. Sometimes I would slip off and talk to the flowers, but I had to be careful that nobody saw me, as I knew they would laugh. When Daddy could afford it he bought us sweets and cakes, or took us to a cinema. When he was out of a job we just walked. He was a forester, so when he did have work he earned good money, and then he would shower us with gifts.

The Mission buildings belonged to two elderly Greek-born ladies, the Misses Curatos, from whom Herzi used to take English lessons. One evening when she was due for her usual lesson, she suddenly developed an acute headache and sent Haim, who was then still living at the Mission, over with a note making her excuses.

We all went to bed early that night, and the next morning we were startled when the postman, in a state of shock, came to tell us that he had found the ladies and their two servants all dead. Sister Olga and Rachel ran over to the house, where a dreadful sight met them. The two sisters lay murdered in their sitting room, and the two maids in a pool of blood in the kitchen. Later it was discovered that the lover of one of the maids had come to rob the house.

Wild rumours spread through the town, and the story reached my father that some of the Mission teachers and children had been murdered. Lina and I were sitting looking out of the window, not knowing quite what had happened, with strict orders not to open the door to any strangers, when suddenly I saw Daddy running like a madman towards the house. When I opened the door he could hardly speak for joy that we were all alive. I believe it was then that he got the heart disease of which he eventually died.

One day Daddy appeared with a lady and asked me what I would think of her as a mother. I answered frankly that I would not like it at all, especially as I had in the meantime become so attached to Sister Olga that I could not think of anyone but her in that role. Whether my reaction had anything to do with it I do not know, but he never did marry again.

Sister Olga showed me all the love and tenderness a mother could give. When I was ill she nursed me with devotion. Her love enveloped me day and night, and she made constant sacrifices on my account. I remember especially one summer in Vulcan. We were on an outing when someone suggested that we should all climb a mountain. Everybody was to go, grown-ups and children. Everyone but me. I was not strong enough for such exertion. Sister Olga volunteered to stay behind to keep me company. I realise now what this must have meant to her, coming as she did from a mountainous country. But instead of enjoying herself with the others, she stayed with me, telling me stories and inventing games to pass the time.

Another summer I was picking mushrooms in the woods when I tripped over a stone and received a bad scratch. There must have been a poisonous mushroom among those I had picked, for I developed blood poisoning and the doctor could not guarantee that I would live. Sister Olga sent a wire to my father and watched over me day and night until the danger was over. One night when she was sleeping beside me I felt a strange power coming from her body, and the next day I took the turn from death to life. I am quite convinced of the reality of this power. No wonder I loved her as I would have loved my own mother, so that one day I asked her to let me call her Mami, and so she has remained for me ever since.

Mami now lives in Israel. When she had to leave Rumania, she asked the Mission to transfer her to Israel where so many of her 'children' are living. It is more than true what Isaiah says in chapter 54 verse 1: "More are the children of the desolate than the children of the married wife." Mami has been an inspiration and an example of devotion and love for many a young girl and boy now scattered all over the world.

One summer in Vulcan, while I was having afternoon tea at Miss Galka's house, I was introduced to a young soldier. He was tall and handsome, and very polite — so polite that he even kissed my hand. At that moment my heart stopped, then jumped and started racing as I had never felt it do before. I had fallen in love. This young man was to become a great missionary and a blessing to many. His name was Isac Feinstein. Through him, many years later, another great missionary was to come to a living faith in the crucified and risen Jesus Christ — Richard Wurmbrand.

Isac Feinstein had been converted through the Church Mission to the Jews, an English mission which was working in Bucharest. After he had finished his military service, he became a travelling salesman, and his journeys often brought him to Galatz. Whenever he was at the Mission, the house echoed with his gay laughter and he always had small attentions to pay to us children.

I noticed Herzi and Mami having long talks with him, and later I learned that they, through the *Israelsmisjonen,* had offered to give him a missionary training, and afterwards work with the Mission. One Easter, he came for a holiday together with his fiancée, a Swiss teacher at one of the C.M.J.'s English schools in Bucharest. Thus I had to bury my first love. It was a little painful, but nobody suspected.

After their marriage the young couple went to Warsaw for training. I think the money spent on this was the best investment the *Israelsmisjonen* ever made. Not only was Feinstein a great missionary, but he was a source of inspiration to all who met him. He had a marvellous sense of humour, which made him a delightful companion at parties and other social occasions. But his greatest gift was his unforgettable way of teaching Christian truths.

A young convert once asked him, "What does the Bible mean by the sin of pride?"

Feinstein answered, "Stop asking silly questions, you idiot."

The young man was angry. Feinstein told him, smiling, "Well, now you know what pride is. It is to mind if somebody insults you."

When asked by another about 'the outer darkness' which Jesus says will be the fate of the wicked, he lit a candle, blew it out and then lit it again. The questioner immediately understood. God is light. God is everywhere. So everywhere there can only be light. Darkness is a place where someone has intentionally blown out the light. A man can rekindle it. But one day Jesus will take away the box of matches. He must rekindle it while he still has the matches.

Feinstein was an exceptional preacher. His sermons were full of illustrations which stick in the mind.

I remember one which he took from Aesop. A horse and an ass, both heavily laden, were walking behind their master. The ass implored his companion to relieve him of his burden, even if only for a little while, or else he might drop dead. The horse refused and the ass died under the weight of his burden. The master then laid the entire load upon the horse. "Well," thought the horse, "it is no more than I deserve for my ill nature in refusing to help my brother in the depth of his distress."

This story often comes to my mind when I think about the indifference of Christians and Jews in the free world towards their brothers worn out by communist persecution. Will they be strong enough to bear the whole burden alone? We can already sing a requiem for the Church in China, and for that of the Sudan. Are we going to allow Christianity to die out in Eastern Europe also?

3

Norway and England

As I GREW older and my faith grew stronger, I longed to be baptised. But I never even dared to breathe a word about this to my family.

Another ambition, which seemed equally unattainable, was to go to school in Norway. Anti-Semitism was rife in Rumania, and we Jewish children suffered from it as much as adults. Mami and Herzi had promised to meet the expenses for sending me to Norway if my father would give his consent, but he was reluctant to let me go so far away. Disappointed as I was, I understood his point of view, and did not insist.

The next year, however, something happened which made him change his mind and realise that if I was to have a good education he would have to let me go.

I had been prepared for my examinations by Aunt Dora, and had got excellent marks in everything but arithmetic, for which the results had not yet come through. We went to Vulcan for the summer, and when we came home in the autumn I still had not heard. Then the blow fell. I had failed — and the mark I had was so bad that I could not take another exam but would have to lose a whole year.

I was not the brightest of pupils when it came to arithmetic,

I knew, but the real reason for the disaster was that I had a Jewish name, and the person who marked our papers was known to be one of the worst anti-Semites in Galatz. The result of my oral examination was good, so I had to have a bad mark for my written work to prevent the possibility of my continuing at school.

I was inconsolable. My father had hoped that at least one of his children should go on to further education, and though Haim had a very good brain he did not care for school. Now he understood what it meant to me, and finally agreed that I should go.

Since both Mami and Herzi were due for home leave, it was arranged that I should travel with them. The days flew by, and I had no time to think about what this journey really implied. That I was not to see my father and sister and brother for many years did not dawn on me. Had I realised it, I might have changed my mind. Eight long years were to pass before I saw them again. Mami and Herzi returned to Norway a couple of times during my stay there. But when they left I was sick with longing for them and my own family, and my home at the Mission at Galatz.

On our way to Norway in that summer of 1928, we attended a congress in Hamburg of the International Hebrew Christian Alliance, whose purpose is to establish a common witness of Jews who believe in Christ to their own people.

In the diaspora, as a rule, Jews who are converted tend to become assimilated with the nation among whom they live, at least in the second generation, often marrying Gentiles. Some of them are very fine Christians, but though they may occasionally witness for Christ to a Jew, they become lost to Jewry. Our people reproach us that when we become Christians we become lost to the Jewish nation, which is very often true. It even happened with the first Christians. In the beginning they were all Jews, but those who remained of them after the destruction of Jerusalem in A.D. 70 were eventually swallowed up by the expanding churches among other peoples.

The Hebrew Christian Alliance is a perhaps romantic attempt to keep Jewish Christians as Jews, and to defend them against anti-Semitism and against anti-Christian prejudice. The ultimate hope of this organisation is to establish a Hebrew Christian church in Israel itself.

The Hamburg congress gave me my first glimpse of this world-wide fellowship of Christian Jews and, young though I was, I immediately found it stimulating. Also at the conference were several young men of whom I did not take a great deal of notice at the time, and who certainly did not pay any attention to a little girl of fourteen. Among them were the present Executive Secretary, the Rev. Harcourt Samuel, Mr. Jacob Pelz, who later became the Secretary in America, and Sir Louis Levinson, the first President of the I.H.C.A. Many years later, I was co-opted as a member of the executive committee of the I.H.C.A., and through the Alliance was able to help Hebrew Christians behind the iron curtain. The I.H.C.A. was one of the instruments in obtaining the release of the Wurmbrands to the West. I have often been brought to marvel at the Lord's wonderful timing. You meet someone you never expect to see again, and in His own time this person will be of the greatest help to you, or to someone dear to you.

We arrived in Norway at the end of July. It was a marvellous experience for me. The country was so beautiful, the people so kind — and the weather so cold!

But the greatest and most wonderful thing that happened to me was my baptism. One Sunday in late August a small group stayed behind in church after the main service, and in their presence I made my promise to God that I would be faithful to Him through my Saviour Jesus Christ.

The pastor who baptised me I had met in Rumania. Two years before, he had visited the Mission, and we had become great friends. Martin Wiig was a very dear man, whom I shall never forget. I am still close to his family through my friendship with his youngest son, Sven. When, after the war, I made up my mind to leave Rumania and return to Norway, it was Sven who helped me to get the papers I needed. During the more than twenty years I have lived in Norway, he and his wife and children have again and again proved the real meaning of friendship. I consider them my 'family' in Norway.

In Oslo it was arranged that I would make my home with Margit Berg, a former missionary in Galatz, and indeed one of the ladies who had received us at the Mission on that first day. Miss Berg now led the Home Mission of the *Israelsmisjonen*. She helped me with my Norwegian, so that within a month I could already understand what was going on in my classroom at the private school I attended. It was not easy, and I had to work very hard to pass my examinations, but at least I knew I would never risk failing just because I was a Jewess. I had heard a lot about democracy, but I was only now for the first time experiencing what it meant.

I enjoyed school, and made many friends both there and at the Mission. Unfortunately what with homesickness, hard work and the long journey to school every day, as well as the cold weather, I became very ill in the winter of 1929, and had to miss a whole year's schooling.

I went into a nursing home for several months, and when I came out I could not face going back to the Mission. The house was dark, and had no garden — how I missed our beautiful garden in Galatz — and besides, Miss Berg and I did not get on too well. She had her own ideas about how young people should behave, as I had about old people. I had a friend named Frieda, a foster-daughter of Herzi's, who lived in Hamar, a little town not far from Oslo. She was a district nurse, and had a flat in the house of an elderly pastor. She invited me to live with her, sharing expenses. I was much happier with this arrangement. Frieda was only fifteen years older than myself, and we became close friends.

In due course I passed my examinations, and returned to Oslo in the autumn of 1931 to attend high school. Here I lived in a hostel with a lot of other young girls. The school was a private one, the only Christian high school in Norway at that time. In my class there were sixteen young men, all destined to go as missionaries to China. These boys deeply impressed me by the quality of their lives, though I never felt any call to be a missionary myself.

Two very happy years passed. I had become used to being independent, was doing well at school, and indulged in rosy dreams about the future. I passed my matriculation and was ready to go to the university. I intended to study medicine, and to go home as a doctor to open a clinic in Galatz.

Then one day I received a heavy blow. The solicitor in charge of my money died suddenly, and it was said that he had been embezzling the funds. I was heartbroken, but there was nothing to be done. Abandoning my hopes of a medical career, I spent the next year learning shorthand and typing, and doing a Bible course in Oslo.

Meanwhile, plans were made for me to go to the Redcliffe Missionary Training College in London, in order to perfect my English. In the autumn of 1934 I left Oslo for Bergen, to take the boat for England.

At Charing Cross station in London I missed the lady who was to meet me and take me to Redcliffe. So I arrived very late, very tired and very shy. I was received by Miss Naish, at that time assistant principal, who introduced me to the other students, mostly British, but some foreigners.

The college buildings stood in a large garden, which at once gave me a feeling of home. The rooms were pleasant and everything seemed to be well organised. But the first meals were a great strain for me. The customs were quite different from what I had been used to. Everyone sat as stiff as a poker at table. You were not supposed even to ask for the salt if you needed it, and wanting a second helping was a crime which I often committed. Not being British, I preferred my tea without milk and sugar, and the others used to tease me about this.

I could not understand the British sense of humour. When

one of the British girls told a joke, I never knew if it was supposed to be funny or not. On the other hand, they found it difficult to understand me. And then there was always the danger of offending one of them.

"You English!" I would exclaim when something struck me as particularly absurd, and they would protest indignantly. Eventually I discovered that some of them were Welsh, or Irish, or Scottish — and this at last cleared the air between us. People from the Continent are not aware of how seriously these national differences are taken in Britain.

But all these things were only trifles compared with the strict daily schedule. From early morning until late at night almost every moment was occupied. Saturday was our day off, and as soon as it was ten o'clock and I had finished my chores I was off like an arrow. Usually I went sight-seeing, and in the end I knew London better than many of the British-born girls. Sometimes I was invited out for the day by English friends; it was interesting to visit an English home, but the etiquette was so different from what I was used to, that I often could not enjoy myself properly, through fear of committing some social blunder.

It was no good coming back on Saturday evening dead tired, because Sunday was our heaviest day of all. Before going to church we usually each had a Sunday School class. After lunch there were open-air meetings, and in the evening we again went to church, or to a meeting where some of the students had to give a talk.

Most of the girls found life in the college very tough. Some gave up after only one term, some after two. Only a few stayed on for the full two years. Originally it was decided that I should remain for one year. This was as much as Mami and Herzi could afford. But though I found the discipline more than hard, I felt that it was the making of my character, and that above all I was learning to know the Lord better. I asked Him to make it possible for me to stay on for a second year, even though I had no call to become a missionary.

He found it necessary to try my faith. My fees had not arrived by the time the summer term was over and I was due to leave for home. Nevertheless, I made up my mind that I would stay on in faith, so I took a job as a nursemaid for the vacation, and in the autumn I returned to Redcliffe.

The money I had earned on my job I mostly used for stamps and church collections. Eventually it came to an end, and now I had to trust the Lord for every penny. If I went to church and had nothing to put in the plate, my fellow students would notice. But the Lord always provided. One Sunday I was in despair, as my pocket was quite empty. On the way to church I saw something shining on the ground. It was a sixpence. Once more I was saved from embarrassment.

If we wanted to go to a meeting during the week, we had to ask permission. There was one meeting which I felt the Lord was urging me to attend. I had no money for the fare, and on the way to the Underground I wondered what would happen if the Lord did not send me the fare after all. I should lose face by returning to the college. But as I entered the station I met an acquaintance who asked me if I had already bought my ticket.

Over Easter I remained at the college, helping with the cleaning. Miss Miall, the principal, asked me to go on an errand, and on the way back my eyes were caught by a shop window full of Easter eggs. My mouth began to water uncontrollably. My whole being craved for chocolate. Never before or since have I felt such a temptation to buy something to satisfy my appetite. But I knew that I must save every penny for whatever needs might arise. On my return to Redcliffe Miss Miall handed me a parcel. It contained a whole pound of delicious chocolate!

What we students dreaded most of all were the Private Interviews — known as P.I.s — with Miss Miall. She was a most lovable person, though very, very strict, who would 'search our hearts and reins' and tell us all about our faults, at the same time showing us the way we should go. I must have been one of the most difficult students the college ever had, as I had very frequent P.I.s – several a term. I know of one girl who did not have more than a handful during her whole two years.

We had to wear uniform — navy blue with white starched collars and dreadful hats. And woe betide us if we ever forgot to take our gloves when we went out for a walk. Even when we went to the swimming baths we had to wear gloves.

We were supposed to have one hour's walk a day. This had to last exactly sixty minutes. If we had walked for only fifty-eight minutes we had to apologise to Miss Miall.

One of the most difficult things was that it was absolutely forbidden to be ill. So far as I was concerned, I several times had to take a day or a few hours off, but I was made to feel it was a great disgrace.

When, over thirty years later, I visited Redcliffe again, things had changed immeasurably. The first thing I noticed was that the students were not wearing uniform — even though it was not Saturday. As soon as Miss Naish became principal, she abolished the uniforms. The rooms were comfortably furnished, and there was more space for the students. On the landing there was even a little cupboard with medicines for those who did not feel well.

But the really important thing, which has remained unchanged since the time when I was a student, is that Redcliffe has continued to train missionaries in the true spirit of God, giving them Bible teaching and training in discipline, and teaching them how to get on with all kinds of people. I have always been extremely grateful to God and to all who helped me to have this training, arduous though it was at the time.

4

Bucharest

AT LONG LAST I could return home. Oh, the joy of it — to see my family again, to hear the old gate still squeaking, to work in the garden once more!

In fact, after eight years of separation I found it very difficult to take up the threads again. Daddy was still the same, but Rachel and Haim, like myself, had grown up, and we had been living in quite different environments, which had left their mark on us all. Haim had just begun his military service, and Rachel, who had married while I was away, was expecting her first baby and had already been divorced. It took some time for us to find each other again.

At the Mission, too, everything seemed to have changed. Here, the changes were very much for the better. The Feinstein family were installed in one of the flats, and the premises echoed with young laughter. People were continually coming and going. There were at least two services every Sunday in the meeting hall which had been formed out of two of the class-rooms, the school having been discontinued. Feinstein was an excellent preacher; he had a beautiful voice and used to sing duets with his wife, who also played the organ. The 'Ebenezer' hall was always filled to the last seat, and on Jewish autumn holidays many people were standing out in the courtyard.

Whereas in the old days the Mission had been frequented only by women and children, now a lot of men came as well. Those who were converted were baptised by Feinstein. He himself belonged to the Brethren, and the Mission was Lutheran, but I never heard one word of discord between him and Mami and Herzi.

Several small rooms had been opened up to form a large hall known as the 'ping pong', where games were played by the young people and parties were held for the whole congregation at Christmas and Easter, and on other notable occasions such as Herzi's seventieth birthday. The hall was also used for evening classes, particularly for courses in English run by Mrs. Feinstein and Herzi. The attic of one of the buildings had been turned into guest rooms, and there was a constant stream of visitors from other towns or from abroad.

Another innovation was the publication of a Christian periodical, *Prietenul* (The Friend), which was shortly followed by another, *Prietenul Copiilor* (The Children's Friend). These were edited by Feinstein. He had also founded a summer camp for young men and boys, in Vulcan. The girls who lived at the Mission did the cleaning, Mami and Aunt Dora looked after the cooking, while Feinstein and Mr. H. L. Ellison from the Church Mission to Jews in Bucharest took Bible studies and prayers. Through these camps several young men were converted and baptised. The conversions also had a side-effect — they supplied husbands for some of the girls at the Mission! There is a passage in the Talmud in which a rabbi says, "In six days God created heaven and earth. On the seventh day He rested. What has He been doing since?" Another rabbi replies, "Planning marriages." He sometimes uses His churches and missions for this purpose!

After a long rest and a holiday at Vulcan, I had to decide what I was going to do for a living. I was offered the chance of taking over all the English teaching at the Mission's evening school, and to expand its courses. This attracted me very much, and I was about to accept gladly when I discovered that there was a condition attached to the offer. I was not to live at the Mission, nor in my father's home.

With two homes already in Galatz, to have to make a third one for myself — to rent a room with strangers — was not acceptable to me. Mami and Herzi were disappointed, and Feinstein was very annoyed. It had been his idea, and jobs were not all that easy to come by, unless you knew people. Feinstein did have business connections, and I thought it would have been easy enough for him to help me find something, since I had had a good education. But he advised me to get a job as a governess. So a governess I became. It was not exactly the fulfilment of my ambitions. But for the moment I had no choice.

I put an advertisement in the papers. At that time there were many wealthy English families in Rumania, working for the oil companies. One of these families answered my advertisement and offered me a job. The husband was English, his wife Rumanian, the daughter of a general.

At the interview I told her I was a Hebrew Christian.

"I've nothing against Jews myself," she assured me, and went on to say that she was glad I was a Christian as well, since I could then teach the children religion.

They lived in the country, near Ploesti, in a beautiful house where I was treated like one of the family. They had two delightful little girls with whom I got on very well. I thought they looked rather sickly when I first arrived, so I put them on a diet which soon improved their health. As time went by, I was entrusted with more and more responsibility in the house. Thus when the family went away for a few days, I was given the keys and had the supervision of the maids. The only person who obviously disliked me was Mrs. Horn's mother, who lived with them, and who seemed to be jealous of me because of the children. Though I did everything I could to pacify her, she seemed to delight in making me feel miserable.

Then one day in 1938 everything changed. A new, anti-Semitic government was elected. The atmosphere in the house became tense and unbearable, and as the days passed I could not even go out for a walk in the village without people shouting after me, "*Jidanca* — dirty Jewess!" The housemaid stopped cleaning my room, and Mrs. Horn did nothing to reprove her. The children, who did not understand what was going on, nevertheless sensed something unusual and took advantage of the situation. As soon as I had put them to bed I would take refuge in my room instead of joining the family in the living room. When one day even Mrs. Horn called me "*Jidanca*", I retorted, "I take it you no longer need the services of a dirty Jewess," and gave in my notice.

Before my month was up, the government fell, to be replaced by a more liberal regime, and almost overnight it seemed, the atmosphere changed again. The children became obedient, the servants polite. Mr. Horn, the only one who had remained friendly throughout, tried to persuade me to stay on, but his wife refused to apologise for her insult, and I left.

I moved to Bucharest, where I got a job with a Jewish family, and began giving English lessons in my spare time. Soon I had so many pupils that I moved to the C.M.J.'s boarding house for foreign teachers. Several of the girls at the Mission school asked me for private lessons, and now and again I stood in for one of the teachers who was ill or on holiday.

I enjoyed teaching, and I liked being in Bucharest, where I made many friends, especially among the Hebrew Christians. My shyness and awkwardness disappeared. I was earning good money, so that I could help my family, which had increased with the birth of my sister's little girl, whom I loved dearly from the first moment I saw her. Christmas, Easter and Whitsun I spent in Galatz, dividing my time between the Mission and my family. In Bucharest I found myself taking a more and more active part in the work and witness of the Hebrew Christian community.

Everyone seemed to be talking, that autumn, about a young Jewish couple who had recently been converted and who were already, I gathered, causing quite a stir by their outstanding Christian witness. I was intrigued by the stories I heard, and very much wanted to meet them, but could not find anyone to introduce us.

"I'd like to get to know the Wurmbrands," I said to my friend Riva Rosenberg, who knew them. "Couldn't you take me to visit them?" But Riva had two small children and found it difficult to get out.

Then one evening in November, at a meeting in the school, I was introduced to a small, vivacious young woman, who looked even more diminutive beside her handsome giant of a husband. Did I have some intuition, at that instant, of the strong ties of friendship which were to bind me to Sabina and Richard Wurmbrand, and the momentous experiences, both good and evil, which we were to share?

Bintzea at once embraced me, and her warm smile went straight to my heart. In the Book of Samuel it is written that "the soul of Jonathan was knit with the soul of David", and that is how it was with Bintzea and me, from the very beginning. Nothing but death can undo our friendship.

Richard, too, impressed me deeply. He was very different from his wife: he struck me as being a serious man who hardly ever smiled, and there was a dignity about him which I felt sure he had acquired since his conversion. The strange thing is that he only learned to smile and laugh many years later during his long period of suffering in prison.

Though the Wurmbrands were living at that time on the outskirts of the city, I saw them frequently. Bintzea was expecting a baby and so did not go out much, but I spent a lot of time round at their place, and our friendship deepened rapidly.

We decided to exchange our knowledge of languages. Bintzea had studied at the Sorbonne, so her French was impeccable. However, after Mihai was born, our lessons had to stop. As soon as we settled down to a session, he would start crying so loudly that you could hear him at the end of the street. The moment we agreed to call it a day, he was quiet. I'm afraid my French is still rudimentary.

Not long after Mihai's birth, the Wurmbrands moved to a more central part of the city, where their home soon became a hub of Christian activity, especially among the Hebrew Christians. There was a large group of us, and most of us were young. At the Mission's school in Olteni Street, the hall normally used for gym was transformed into a chapel on Sundays or on midweek evenings, and we would meet there for services, Bible studies and women's meetings. After a time I started a Sunday School. Richard was allowed to preach now and then. He was already an inspiration to us all, but the great things had not yet begun to happen.

In Galatz, too, changes had taken place. A Norwegian pastor, Magne Solheim, came to take over the work there, and Feinstein and Mami went to open a new work in Jassy, near the Russian border — a fateful move, as it turned out. In the meantime, in addition to her other work, Mami had opened a school for nurses at the Jewish hospital in Galatz, and later in Jassy. So far as I know, these were the first schools of their kind in Rumania. She continued to supervise this work until she moved to Bucharest during the war, after the great disaster had befallen Rumanian Jewry.

In 1939, Rumania was forced to cede to Russia Bessarabia and part of Bukovina, while Hungary took over Transylvania, and Bulgaria part of Dobrodja. King Carol II was deposed, and his son Michael became King for the second time in his short life.

Many of us had relatives and friends in the parts of the country which were given up. Thus my brother Haim, who was doing his military service in Cernauti, chose to remain there, little knowing in what oceans of suffering he would be immersed before we met again. There was a nominal convention that the borders should be open for three days so that anybody who wanted to could cross in either direction. Many made use of this convention, but when Rumania eventually entered the war, those Jewish families whose relatives had preferred to go to Russia suddenly disappeared during the night and were never seen again. Two of my most promising students, a couple by the name of Barsky, disappeared in this way. One afternoon there was nobody to answer the bell when I arrived for the usual lesson and from that time nobody heard anything more about them. But Mrs. Barsky's mother had been one of those who had crossed the border into Russia.

When the war broke out, Rumania, though still technically neutral, was gradually invaded by German military personnel. We Jews made a point of demonstratively crossing the street whenever we saw a German soldier. After a few months we had to give this up — there were more German than Rumanian soldiers in the streets. But we would still get up from our seats in the trams and buses if a German sat next to us.

There had not yet been any steps taken against the Jews, but we had a foreboding of what was coming, and we were very frightened. Swastikas appeared everywhere on the fences, and the newspapers published anti-Semitic articles. At that time nobody knew what was happening to the Jews in Germany, but when the Germans invaded Poland many thousands of Jews fled to Rumania, from where they went to Palestine.

Now the Rumanian Fascists, the Greenshirts, began to feel their strength and tried to seize power in the country. They were opposed by another Fascist group headed by General Antonescu. In Bucharest there was a rebellion which lasted for three days. The Greenshirts killed many of the Rumanian intelligentsia, among them the world-renowned Professor Nicolai Jorga. His and other dead bodies were thrown into the streets or dumped in the woods. The bodies of murdered Jews were hung up in the slaughter house along with the carcases of cattle. Synagogues were burned down. Nobody went out into the streets except on urgent business. Machine-guns shattered the silence, and many fires lit up the city.

Then on the fourth day the rebellion stopped as suddenly as it had started. General Antonescu, who was later to form a government, put down the Greenshirts, though not before they had thrown petrol over the soldiers and burned many alive. Corneliu Codreanu, the leader of the Greenshirts, and many with him were arrested, and peace and order again reigned in the city. We Jews did not feel very safe — all the same, the situation had slightly improved.

At the English Mission there was a new leader, the Rev. Roger Allison. He had worked with the C.M.J. in Warsaw, but had had to flee when the Germans invaded Poland. Since he knew no Rumanian, he used Richard as a preacher. Richard has always been a powerful speaker, but those early sermons of his were not very biblical. He would take his illustrations from science, history, geography — anything but the Bible. I once took him to task about this.

"The Bible is full of stories and events which you could use as illustrations. Why don't you?"

To my astonishment he calmly replied, "Because it isn't necessary," and continued as before.

In years to come I was to hear other words from him. He learned to know and love the Word of God. I have heard him rebuke a guest who dared to make a joke during a meal.

"We are in a Christian home here," he said sternly, "and I don't allow anybody to speak of anything but of Jesus Christ."

Thus we who had been Christians for many years watched the daily growth in faith of Richard and Bintzea. Soon they outgrew us and became giants in the Kingdom of God.

Another thing which used to irritate me about Richard's sermons in the early days was their length. They never lasted less than three-quarters of an hour. So when, one evening, he stopped preaching after only twenty minutes, I could not believe my ears. He stepped down from the platform, leaving Mr. Allison to dismiss the congregation after a hymn and a short prayer.

As I made my way towards the door when the service had ended, I could see that something unusual was going on. There was a group of Greenshirts present, who had certainly not come to hear the Word of God! I saw Mr. Allison talking to one of them in the courtyard. But as he knew no Rumanian and the Greenshirt no English, the conversation was not making much progress. I joined them, hoping to be of some help.

"Wurmbrand. Where is Wurmbrand? Where is Wurmbrand?" the man was shouting, barely pausing for an answer.

When Mr. Allison replied, quite truthfully, that he did not know, the man lost his temper and took us both off to the police station for interrogation. Here we were met by a whole gang of Greenshirts, who literally howled at us — one even showed me the revolver he was going to shoot me with if I did not tell them where Richard was. He had, in fact, as we discovered later, slipped out of the hall through a door hidden behind a curtain.

This was my first experience of arrest, but strangely I was not afraid. Remembering Paul and Silas in prison at Philippi, I asked Mr. Allison to read me something from the Bible, thinking that, since our jailers were listening, it would do them no harm to hear the Scriptures. We sang some hymns, too, and had a regular service. As soon as the Greenshirts realised what we were up to, they ordered us to be quiet.

Several others of our people were brought in, but released after a short interrogation. At last we too were allowed to go. One of the Greenshirts followed me closely all the way back to the school. I was certain he was going to shoot me, but he only wanted to see where I was going. When I got indoors, I had a fit of hysterics, and it took me some time to recover. I am quite certain that if Richard had not hurriedly left the service, he would have been shot. As it was, he came home cheerfully late that night, happy to have tricked the Greenshirts.

5

War

In June 1940 Rumania, at the instigation of Germany, declared war on Russia and sent troops over the Dniester. Simultaneously, persecution of the Jews broke out. In Jassy, all the Jewish men, young and old alike, were rounded up and either killed on the spot or locked up together in cattle trucks. The trains were shunted to and fro, but nobody was allowed to go near them to bring relief to the unhappy prisoners, who were calling out for water. The gutters of the town ran red with Jewish blood, and only a very few who were able to hide escaped. Isac Feinstein was among those who were arrested and put into a train, where he died of suffocation — one of 12,000 victims.

Mami was at the hospital and knew nothing of what was going on at the Mission. When she learned about Feinstein, it was too late. She could probably have saved him, had she been at the Mission house. Later she was fully occupied in sheltering all those who came to her; she was able to hide about a hundred people in the cellar, at the risk of her own life, until the danger was over.

In Bucharest we were appalled when we heard what had happened. Richard set about organising ways of bringing out

the survivors. He persuaded an influential Rumanian Christian
to get the Hebrew Christians placed under arrest and brought
to the capital under escort. On their arrival, the arrest order was
torn up and they were allowed to go free. Richard himself went
at great risk to Jassy to fetch Mrs. Feinstein and her six children, the youngest of whom was only two. To arrange housing
and rations for all these people was a formidable problem, but
somehow he fixed this too.

A few days later we learned that many of the Jews in the
occupied territories of Bessarabia and Bukovina who had not
already been deported had been massacred, among them
Bintzea's parents and sisters. Haim, with his wife and baby,
were deported to Moghilev in German-occupied Russia.

With the declaration of war, the English missioners and
teachers were expelled and the C.M.J.'s premises in Bucharest
were turned into a hospital. I now had to find myself a new
home. Richard had some time ago given up a good job to work
full time for the Mission. He had started a youth work, and
organised open-air meetings. Now he had to take over full pas-
toral responsibility. He was frequently away from home, visiting the sick, or inviting people to the meetings, and we always
gave a sigh of relief when he returned safely.

Bintzea, too, in spite of her personal grief and the increasing
danger, showed herself an active evangelist. Along with a group
of young Christian girls she would go out into the streets and
talk to passers-by, pleading with them to be reconciled to God.
Bintzea is an excellent preacher. She had studied law at the
Sorbonne, and I often tell people that the world lost a great
advocate when she gave up her studies. But if she could not
plead in the law courts, she was still pleading — with unbelievers to accept Christ, with believers to give their lives to His
service. I have never met a more effective pleader than
Bintzea.

Since all public gatherings of the Hebrew Christians were
now forbidden, services were held secretly at the Wurmbrands'
tiny two-roomed flat. It had the advantage of being on the

ground floor, so that when the police came, which happened several times, Richard could keep them talking at the front door while we disappeared through the windows.

It was not only on Sundays that we met. There were also meetings on weekday evenings. Richard and Bintzea were our spiritual parents, and nothing could keep us away. Richard was breaking the law by baptising Jews in his home — the government had decreed that no Jews were to be baptised. A true act of faith was called for on the part of both the convert and the pastor, as each knew very well that they were risking their liberty and perhaps their lives, if they were caught.

From time to time, Jewish Christians were arrested, or taken in for questioning. Richard was arrested a couple of times, but they could never pin anything on him — except the only crime of which he could not repent: that of being a Jew.

I, too, found myself taken one day for interrogation by the police. In the course of the questioning, they produced papers which purported to prove that I was a German.

"No," I insisted firmly, to their astonishment, "I'm a Jewess."

It was a risky assertion during the Nazi occupation, but I believe my truthfulness that day saved my life after the war, when the Germans were hunted down like animals.

It was a heavy blow for me when I was conscripted, along with other Jewish women, for compulsory labour. I had been the only member of my family who was earning, and had been sending all I could spare to my father and Rachel and her small daughter, Lisa. I had even managed to send a little money to my brother in Byelorussia. But he wrote telling me not to deprive myself on his account, as what I sent would hardly buy them a loaf of bread, and it only meant less for the rest of the family.

I continued giving English lessons in the evenings, after a full day's work, in order to earn some sort of living. Inevitably, the strain became too much for me. I developed tuberculosis.

Bintzea and Richard generously took me into their home to

look after me, since I could not get into a hospital. A Jew could not be accepted in a state hospital, and all the Jewish hospitals had been taken over by the Nazis. As the Wurmbrands had only two small rooms, it meant that I had to move into their bedroom during the day, into their own bed, while at night I would sleep in the tiny entrance hall which served as their living room.

Bintzea nursed me with the patience of an angel. It was the winter of 1941 — the worst for many years. Food was desperately short, but almost every hour Bintzea would bring me something to eat or drink. I had no appetite because of my illness, and the knowledge that so many people, including my own family, were starving, made it even worse. I wept and protested, all to no avail. Bintzea would stay with me until everything was eaten up.

I was also worried about Mihai. Supposing he caught my illness? Bintzea and Richard accepted this risk. Someone had to care for me, and they would not leave this privilege to others.

Mihai and I were great friends. He was a lively child, very intelligent and a great rascal. He would come and talk to me as I lay in bed, and I do not know which of us enjoyed the conversations the most. I love children, and greatly missed my niece Lisa now that we were unable to travel to visit one another. I would tease Mihai by calling him a scamp, which upset his dignity. "If you call me scamp I will not come to see you," he told me, and I had to promise him earnestly not to do so.

When I got better and could kiss him without endangering his health, I would play a game of telling him he had a button instead of a nose. This greatly worried him, and he would invite me to feel that it really was a nose. I would kiss it and as he looked at me with great anxious eyes, would assure him gravely that it was in fact a nose. This act would be played out over and over again. In spite of his intelligence, Mihai was sometimes very naïve, a trait which he has inherited from his father.

Though Richard is the greatest man I have ever met, and though he has had more opportunities than most people to learn about the weaknesses of human nature, he can still be extraordinarily trusting. And it is just this quality, in my opinion, which enhances his greatness.

We saw a good example of his naïvety that winter. An Orthodox priest called on us one day to say that he was organising help for the Jews who had been deported to Moghilev. Several members of our community were there, as well as my brother.

I lay in bed listening to the conversation in the next room; something about the priest's voice made me uneasy. I called Richard in.

"That man," I said. "I don't trust him. Are you sure he's genuine?"

"Don't be silly," retorted Richard. "Of course he's genuine. He's a priest, isn't he, and he's risking his life to help Jews." He had not yet learned how much wickedness a priest's robe can sometimes hide.

"All the same, I'm not happy about it," I insisted, but Richard would not listen.

I peeped through the doorway at our visitor. It was no use. I just did not like the man.

However, since the others were all enthusiastically gathering things together, I too gave way. We literally undressed ourselves so as to send as much as possible. A woman who happened to be visiting stripped off her warm woollen vest, and put it in the trunk which was soon overflowing. I myself had a small suitcase containing some knitting wool which I had bought in better days, and together with knitting needles and my best clothes this too found its way into the trunk. The priest departed, with our wishes of God speed, and we never saw him again. Neither did our people get a stitch of the clothing we sent them.

With the coming of summer, my health improved, and I was eventually strong enough to move into a room of my own. I continued to see a lot of the Wurmbrands, since during the months I had spent in their home we had grown very close. Now that Bintzea no longer had to nurse me, she was able to go out more, to visit the sick and others in need of help. Whenever I could, I would try to have a good meal waiting for her and Richard when they came in. Like many intellectual women, Bintzea is not particularly domesticated, and looks on cooking as a waste of time. But when the table was attractively laid, perhaps with a bowl of flowers in the centre, and there was something good to eat, both she and Richard could relax and we enjoyed each other's company over a leisurely meal.

In spite of the fact that they were so busy, and that their small flat was always open to anyone in trouble so that they could rarely be alone, they did not allow other things to crowd out their family life.

It was amusing to see tall Richard, making himself even taller by raising his chin, clap his hands and say to his wife, "Bintzea, come and kiss me." While Bintzea, who does not even come up to his shoulder, would have to climb on a chair, stand on tiptoe and pull down his face before she could reach him. This was a favourite party trick which amused us all.

Richard adored Mihai, and always made time to play with him, to tell him stories and especially to talk to him — not baby talk, but serious conversation. From the time he was five years old, Mihai could not go to sleep without first having read something in bed, and Richard provided him with good books.

But though a devoted father, he could also be very strict. I once made the mistake of telling him when Mihai had been particularly naughty, and he gave him such a spanking that whatever offence Mihai committed after that I never told on him again. Bintzea was too soft-hearted, so Mihai often played up to her, but he never dared to do it with his father. So when I hear Richard telling people what an angelic child Mihai was, I have a quiet laugh to myself. He was a regular rascal, always up to mischief. But he was also an extremely generous child, always giving away his toys and goodies, and from an early age he was very religious.

As the war wore on, life in Bucharest became daily more burdensome, especially for us Jews. Our ration cards bore a distinctive mark, which meant that we were not allowed to do our shopping before ten o'clock, by which time nearly everything was sold out. Should we find anything left in the shops, we had to pay double the price and get only half the ration. We were put under curfew after eight o'clock at night, so that those of us who did extra work in the evenings were cut off even from this source of support for our families.

At least we were spared the bombing. The Russians had flown over Bucharest once or twice at first, but had not dropped any bombs; this was before they began receiving help from the Americans. They concentrated their raids on the cities nearer their frontiers.

In spite of everything, our congregation was growing. When Richard first started working at the English Mission, it had consisted mostly of Jews and Hebrew Christians. As his reputation as a preacher spread, many Rumanians left their own churches to join us, the Jewish outcasts. Soldiers who had been called upon to shoot Jewish civilians, came to seek from Richard a word of pardon and guidance.

There were also unbelievers in search of God. Richard, normally an impatient man who wants everything done at once, if not sooner, showed with these seekers an amazing patience. He could explain the Gospel to the simplest minds in such a way that they could often grasp the essentials better than an intellectual person. I was sometimes shocked at his methods, though.

One day he came home radiant.

"S. has been converted!" he announced.

We pressed him for details.

"I made him get down on his knees, and wouldn't let him get up until he had accepted Christ."

This drastic treatment worked. After thirty years S. is still a believer, and a pillar of his church.

The women sometimes came for other reasons than to hear the sermons! The first time I had met Richard, I had been struck by his good looks. He was tall, fair-haired and blue-eyed, a rare combination in that part of the world. I was reminded of the description of Saul in the Old Testament: "He was higher than any of the people from his shoulders upwards." Inevitably, there were women who were attracted to the preacher rather than his message, and who vied for his attention. But they were wasting their time. Richard is utterly devoted to Bintzea, and restless whenever she is not near him.

All the same, the dangers were there. One of his most persistent admirers was Vera, a refugee from Poland. Though she was married, she made no secret of the fact that she was bored with her husband. When Richard was near to a breakdown due to overwork, and was ordered a complete rest, Vera invited him to spend the days at her house, where he could relax in comfort, away from all the coming and going of their own flat.

Richard might be immune to the more obvious feminine wiles, but he was human enough to appreciate kindness and attention, and artless enough not to notice that they could be a means to an end. As an observer — but a loving and compassionate one — I could see that a tricky situation was developing. But did I have any right to interfere?

I made it a particular matter for prayer. Then one night I woke suddenly at about two o'clock, with Richard and Bintzea very much on my mind. At last I got out of bed and on to my knees, and prayed for them the night through. The next day I was at their flat when Vera called, and I could see instantly that the crisis was over. Vera had given up the struggle.

Years later, I learned that, that night, Richard and Bintzea had been awakened by a knocking on their bedroom window, and had distinctly heard my voice calling to them. So strong were the ties of our friendship.

In the autumn of 1943 I again fell ill, this time with scarlet fever. Once again there was the problem of getting into hospital. My Jewish doctor could not get me admitted, so I went to a Rumanian doctor, but he could not hospitalise me because I was a Jew. In the end, I walked to the biggest hospital in Bucharest, and this time they kept me there because I was a public danger.

Conditions were appalling. For the first few days I was kept in a room in the basement for observation. I passed the time watching the fat cockroaches crawling over the floor and the furniture. At night, I had to cover my water glass in case I should find one of the loathsome creatures drowned in it when I had a drink. I was given no medicine; in fact I had not so much as an Aspirin until Bintzea came to visit me.

After some days I was moved into a children's ward. As I was not very ill, I was able to help nurse them. There was practically no medical care, and little in the way of comforts. Sick children had to carry their own used chamber-pots to the toilets to empty them, walking barefoot on the concrete floor. One small girl was crying bitterly with pain in her ear. I had nothing to give her, but I could not stand seeing her suffer. In the end I pretended to dissolve a tablet in a glass of water and gave it to her to drink. She was quiet for an hour or two, but afterwards the earache returned. When I tried the same trick again, it no longer worked.

I was nearly well when I had a relapse and almost died. I experienced an immense curiosity to know what death was like, and can honestly say that I was a little disappointed when I came back to life. A new dimension had opened up for me. There is a Jewish legend which tells that the angel of death has many eyes. If he comes to a death bed and sees that he has arrived too early, he gives the sick man one of his eyes. A person who has been very close to death sees more than other men.

They moved me into a two-bedded room, whose other occupant was a Rumanian schoolteacher who kept saying hopefully,

"I wonder if the Germans have finished off Stalingrad yet." I never answered, hoping with all my heart that they had not. When I was at last discharged, Stalingrad was still in Russian hands.

6

Armistice

So far, Bucharest had experienced few air raids.

From time to time the sirens were tested, always with plenty of warning beforehand. So that when, at eleven o'clock on the morning of the 4th of April 1944, all the sirens in the city began wailing at once, we took little notice. I was visiting one of my students at her office at the time, and we got on with what we were doing.

About an hour later, they started up again. We looked at each other, shrugged — probably just another rehearsal. All at once the earth began to shake with violent explosions. One look at the sky showed us what we were in for. As we ran for the shelter, all hell was let loose above us.

The raid lasted for almost an hour, and when we emerged after the all-clear had sounded, things did not at first look too bad. On my way to the tram stop, I had to pass the Royal Palace. I saw that it was standing untouched. But just across the square, the Athene Palace Hotel, which was the German headquarters, was blazing furiously, watched by a jubilant crowd.

"Look!" they shouted gleefully. "The Anglo-Americans have not touched us, they have only clobbered the Germans!"

The trams were not running, so I had to walk the whole way. For days we were without electricity, and worse, without water. Later we learned that the raid had destroyed a whole section of the city, and there had been many casualties.

From now on, Bucharest and the vital parts of Rumania, where the oil wells were, were subject to daily raids. The British and Americans used to come over at eleven o'clock precisely. The only really bomb-proof shelter in the city was the one under the National Bank, and by nine o'clock a queue had already formed of people carrying bags and attaché cases, making sure of a place when the raid started.

The Wurmbrands used a shelter of sorts near their home. Richard regularly used to offer up a prayer for the safety of the shelterers, a practice which, while it brought comfort to some, infuriated others, and once caused him to be arrested. He was released after a short interrogation, having been charged with subversive propaganda. He had prayed for endangered Rumania, for the Germans, but also for the Jews and the Allies.

A day came when several hours had passed and he had still not come home. I had gone over to see if they were all right, and found Bintzea, who had stayed in the flat that day, so ill with worry, she could scarcely stand. As our anxiety increased, we went out in search of him, only to be met at one police station after another with the same answer: "He is not here." I had to lead Bintzea by the hand, she was so weak.

Finally we gave up and went home. As we opened the door, Richard got up from a chair.

"Where on earth have you been?" he asked. "I was getting worried."

Bintzea nearly fainted.

"Where have *you* been?" I countered. "We've been looking for you all over Bucharest."

"Oh," said Richard cheerfully, "I've been having a wonderful time." And he proceeded to tell us what a marvellous opportunity he had had to witness for Christ to the police who had arrested him.

Poor Bintzea! It was a good thing she did not know then what life had in store for her. Better still! She knew she had a wonderful Saviour, who was to prove His power in His faithful servants during the critical times through which they were to live.

Two momentous things happened to me that spring of 1944. I got engaged: and my brother came home from Russia.

My fiancé, Jacob, was a member of our congregation, a Hebrew Christian like myself. We planned to get married in the summer.

Haim's return was completely unexpected. I had had a post card from him early in the year — in his handwriting, but signed with another name. I could not understand it. I knew he was far away in a German concentration camp, and though I had continued to pray for him, in my heart I had counted him as dead. We had heard rumours that the Jews in these camps were dying like flies. A couple of days later, I had a letter from my father telling me that he too had heard from Haim; that he was well and living in Cernauti, which was once again in the hands of the Rumanians.

Some weeks afterwards, my fiancé came back from a trip to Galatz, looking mysterious.

"How are Daddy and Rachel?" was the first thing I wanted to know.

"Fine. But I'll give you all the news in a moment. Get your coat on, and we can talk on the way."

"Where are we going?"

"Bintzea wants you to go round to her place at once."

"Is something wrong?" My thoughts flew to Richard and arrest.

"Nothing's wrong." He grinned maddeningly. "On the contrary."

"I wish you'd tell me."

"I can't, it's a surprise."

I continued to pester him until he gave in.

"All right, I'll tell you." He was positively beaming with pleasure. "Your brother's waiting to see you."

"Haim!"

I broke into a run, calling over my shoulder to Jacob to let us be alone together. Haim must have felt the same, as he was waiting for me in the small entrance hall. We fell into each other's arms, and I smothered him with kisses, crying for joy, while he just held me tight without saying a word. What could one say to a sister when one had literally returned from the dead?

When we were at last able to speak, Haim gave me a present — ten eggs. He had not only come back from the dead, he was also in a position to give me such a magnificent present!

News of his return spread quickly. People crowded into the house to congratulate me. Overcome with so much emotion, I all of a sudden felt completely exhausted, and fell asleep just where I was in the middle of the room.

Haim had escaped from Russia on a German tank. He had made his way to Cernauti, and from there had walked most of the way to Galatz, as he had no identification papers, and if the Rumanians had discovered where he came from he would have been arrested as a communist. That was why he had come on to Bucharest. It was too risky to stay in Galatz. The problem now was where to hide him. I took him back to my own room, hoping that the three old ladies who owned the house would not discover his presence.

As spring and summer advanced, the air raids grew heavier. The defence systems had been caught quite unprepared, and it often happened that bombs were falling before the alarm sounded. In the end we learned to tell the difference between the German and the Allied planes by the sound they made.

If a raid caught us on a Sunday, in the middle of a service, we stayed where we were, and turned the service into a prayer meeting. None of our community was wounded or killed during these raids.

One Sunday morning, in a particularly heavy raid, we were kneeling in prayer in the small room, when I felt a movement beside me and opened my eyes, thinking somebody might be ill. What I saw shocked me. Two of our young people, oblivious of their surroundings, knelt close together, apparently held in some sort of ecstasy or trance.

We were a very close-knit community, almost like a family, so we knew all about each other's lives. The young man was David, for whom Richard had great hopes as a possible future leader. He was highly intelligent, though inclined to be a bit flighty with the girls. At present he was engaged to a girl called Mary, for the second time, having once before broken off their engagement to become engaged to someone else. Now he appeared to be getting dangerously involved with yet another girl. It occurred to me that Mary had been looking rather miserable recently, but I had been so preoccupied with my own love that I had not taken much notice.

Richard, as pastor, intervened swiftly in the situation. He offered David help with his education and an eventual job at the Mission if he would marry Mary and settle down. In this Richard showed an uncharacteristic lack of judgment. He was too trusting. David was to cause him much suffering and heartache in years to come.

Jacob and I married in the summer, and moved to Galatz, where both our families lived. It was a relief to be away from the bombing.

As the days passed, it became increasingly obvious that some sort of disaster had overtaken the German army. A constant stream of soldiers, dirty, wounded and tired, their uniforms torn and crumpled, was passing through the town — westwards! In the distance we could hear the Russian guns coming nearer every day.

Jacob and I were working at an orphanage on the outskirts of the town. On the 23rd of August, I was visiting Herzi and some recently married girls at the Mission, when one of the new husbands came rushing out into the garden, shouting, "It's all over!" It had just been announced on the radio that Rumania was asking Russia for an armistice.

We were running back to the house to hear this wonderful news for ourselves when we met one of the German pastors who lived in a part of the Mission premises requisitioned by the Nazis. We told him the news. I can still see his face: he turned completely green, tried to say something but had to swallow several times before he at last found his voice and croaked, "It's impossible!" We invited him in to hear the radio — but this was asking too much. As he turned away, his back view looked exactly like a dog slinking off after a scolding from its master.

By the time we got inside the house, the electricity had been cut off, and we could not discover what was happening. Jacob, who had heard the news in town, came at once to fetch me. We hurried off to the orphanage to prepare a shelter, and stock it with food, water, candles and blankets. Jacob was afraid the Germans would take their revenge by bombing the town, though they had promised to withdraw without incident.

He was right. Within a few hours, Galatz was under heavy bombardment, both from the ground and the air. The Russians were on the other side of the Danube, the Germans in the air. The noise was hellish. We took the children down to the shelter and tried to calm them with stories and singing.

In the morning we found a big crack in the cellar ceiling, and we had to work hard all day digging trenches for a new shelter. As evening came on, we took the children out into the field and covered them with blankets, hoping the Germans would not see us, as there was a full moon. I noticed that Nicu, a little deaf and dumb boy, was missing. As I made my way back to the house with two of the older children, we were caught in a new wave of bombs. In the middle of all this we saw two motor cyclists approaching. I thought our last hour had come, but they were Rumanian soldiers on duty. Inside the house, Nicu was sleeping peacefully, oblivious to the pandemonium around him!

From the height on which the orphanage stood we could see fires all over the town. As we stood there watching on the second day, there was a sudden enormous flash, and then the explosion came. It seemed as if all the birds in Galatz were flying shrieking above our heads. The air around us quivered as though it were alive with terror. What could have happened?

The Germans had destroyed the arsenal. After the first big blast it appeared as if the whole town was exploding. That was how the Germans kept their word to withdraw without harming the population. We heard afterwards that they had been going from shelter to shelter, shooting all the people they could find.

On the third night the Russian parachutists arrived, and by the morning of the 26th all was comparatively quiet. Jacob and I went into the town to try to discover what had happened to our families. Huge fires were burning everywhere, and some streets were so enveloped in smoke that we had to make long detours. Houses had been blown up, trees uprooted, and, worst of all, dead bodies were lying all over the streets. There was not a soul about. It seemed we were the only people to have risked leaving our homes.

Then in the distance I saw a man coming towards us. He was still some way off, and half hidden by the smoke, but he made a familiar movement and I recognized my father. At the same moment he saw me, and we both started running. When we met, he flung his arms round me and would not let me go, all the time sobbing like a child, and repeating my name over and over again.

We made our way to the Mission, where they were all safe. So were Jacob's people. But we had no way of knowing what was happening in the rest of the country. All means of communication had been cut. Later, we heard that there had been street fighting in Bucharest, where the Germans had been driven off house by house and man by man. As soon as the street fighting stopped, my brother set out on foot for Galatz and reached the town five days later. It was a great moment when our little family was reunited after so many years.

So far as Rumania was concerned, the war was over. We Jews rejoiced at the prospect of regaining the dignity of human beings: no longer were we to be like cattle driven off to be slaughtered.

Galatz burned for more than a week. When at last it was possible to go out, we were met everywhere by destruction. The obliteration of the port was complete. There was not one whole building or quay standing. Sign boards creaked in the breeze, and the moaning and wailing of the wind sounded like evil spirits. A sinister atmosphere pervaded the whole town. At sunset, people left the streets. Women did not go out alone, even in the day time. The Russians had started looting, raping, robbing, even murdering — in broad daylight. Even the joy of the Jews was rapidly transformed into a dull anxiety over what the future might have in store for us. We Hebrew Christians were sceptical. Richard had warned us that the communists were no better than the Nazis. Had not Stalin liquidated all his leading Jewish comrades? It was no secret that their final aim was to destroy all religion. It seemed likely that more hard times lay ahead.

7

The Coming of Communism

"THANK THE LORD you're safe!" Bintzea and I hugged one another in mutual relief.

Jacob had felt that we ought to get back to Bucharest, and we had somehow achieved the journey. The bridge over the Danube had been destroyed. After hours of waiting, we had made the crossing to Braila in a rowing boat. When we eventually got to the train, it was filled to overflowing with Russian soldiers, and Jacob had to push me into a carriage through the window.

But we had arrived, and were glad to find that all our friends were safe — and also that there were not quite so many Russian soldiers about!

The Mission lost no time in swinging into action. Richard and Bintzea moved into a bigger house, with a large room where we could hold our meetings. Publication of *Prietenul* started up again, and we also printed gospels in Russian. Anyone who could speak any Russian was mobilised to hand them out to the soldiers in the streets. This led to many contacts with Russians who wanted to know more about Christianity. The open air meetings were resumed, and our Sunday services were so crowded that people had to stand in the yard, which was often crammed too.

The German minority among the population, who had hitherto been the privileged ones, now had the tables turned on them. Many had fled with the withdrawing army, but tens of thousands still remained, to find themselves a target for both the Rumanian authorities and the Russian army.

When they had been the proud conquerors, we had avoided them as if they were lepers, considering it to be beneath our Jewish dignity to come into contact with anyone who might be a Nazi. Now, in the time of their defeat, we showed them love. Many of them were hidden in Hebrew Christian homes, though this meant deadly danger. Richard organised a group of us to take care of some Germans and try to get them to safety. I was given charge of two ladies, who were hidden in an attic for about two weeks. Every day I took them food, making sure I was not followed, as there was a death penalty for anyone found helping German soldiers, and these girls had been employed as clerks by the army.

When things seemed to have quietened down a bit, I handed my charges over to the German Evangelical Church. It was tricky getting them across the city, but they were careful not to speak to the tram conductor as they handed over their fare — their accent could have betrayed them — and in the street they walked about fifteen paces behind me. When we got to the church, I rang the bell, watched while they were taken inside, and quickly disappeared. I never heard what became of them later. Not all those we tried to help could be got to safety. Some were arrested and sent to Russia.

This was our first experience of secret work of this nature, and it was to prove valuable training for us in later years. Several of us were involved, but as long as it lasted nobody knew who was taking care of whom. We were also learning to use secrecy in our work among the Russian soldiers.

Even before the armistice was a fact, the Jews who had

survived the hell of the concentration camps began to return
Among them were a great many children who had lost both
their parents and had nobody to turn to. Our meeting room
became a dormitory, with straw mattresses all over the floor,
where homeless youngsters could stay for a night or two before
going on to search for some member of their family. I remember particularly a moving meeting between a boy and a girl who
discovered that they were brother and sister. Neither had
known that the other had survived.

The great problem was how to feed these children. As was
the case all over Europe at the end of the war, food was terribly
short. Just when we were beginning to hope to fill our bellies
once more, a drought hit the greater part of the country. We
were now learning what it really meant to starve. We had ration
cards, but there was nothing to buy with them. Food could only
be got at black market prices. Over the next two years, hundreds of thousands were to die of famine.

The Mission had been sent food parcels from Sweden and
Switzerland — tinned foods, sugar, powdered soup — but there
remained the question of something more substantial. Bread
was not to be had anywhere. Our staple diet was maize meal, of
which we made a kind of porridge called *mamaliga*. So we had
mamaliga for breakfast, dinner and supper — if we were lucky
enough to have three meals a day. It became known that anyone
in need could find something to eat at the Wurmbrands'.
Bintzea would never touch anything that she could give to
others. I have seen her eat *mamaliga* and onion when I knew
for certain that there was more substantial and nourishing food
in the house.

Six children turned up on the doorstep one day, in an indescribably filthy state, ragged and full of lice, their bodies swollen with malnutrition, their eyes wise beyond their years.
Richard and Bintzea at once took these waifs to their hearts,
washed them, fed them and clothed them.

They were desperately in need of medical care. Twelve-
year-old Milo was no bigger than a child of seven. Richard's

doctor somehow found him some hormone injections to make him grow. Milo was a scamp, full of high spirits. One of his favourite expressions was, *"Eih hob hartzeveitik* – I'm heart-broken," said with a beaming smile when he got what he wanted. Betty, the eldest, suffered from sinusitis, and had to have a painful operation.

Ruth was everybody's pet. She was the youngest, a beautiful child of eight. One terrible day, Ruth disappeared. We grew frantic as the days passed and she did not return. Then we learned that she had been kidnapped by some of the Mosaic Jewish community who were angry that Richard and Bintzea wanted to adopt the children and give them a Christian up-bringing.

Richard tried in every way possible to get Ruth back, but in vain. Then one day when I was out in the yard, a small dishevelled figure came running through the gate, her face so smeared with tears and dirt that I failed at first to recognize her. Ruth had somehow managed to escape from her captors and had found her way home.

Richard was threatened with a law suit to decide the custody of the children. However, a few days later, a new regulation was announced. All orphan children who had come out of the former German-occupied territories were either to be returned to Russia or to be sent on to Palestine. The Wurmbrands had no choice. They could not give the children to the communists. They fitted them out as well as possible, and saw them off on a liner for Palestine. When the news came that the *Bul-Bul* had sunk in the Black Sea and there were no survivors, Bintzea shut herself in her bedroom, and Richard's eyes were alter-nately filled with tears or as wild as an animal's that had lost its cubs.

The Russians, after having conquered Rumania, now took over Hungary. We heard that the brethren there were in des-perate need. In those days travel, particularly to another country, was almost impossible. The trains were crowded with Russian troops, and there could be great danger in travelling with them. Bintzea was determined to go to Budapest, and she found a way. She climbed on to the roof of a train and travelled the whole distance in that position. We were all shocked that Richard allowed her to go. But where God's work was concerned he never considered anybody, least of all his family.

Since there was no talking Bintzea out of her decision, we held special prayer meetings to ask the Lord to look after her on the way and return her to us with her task fulfilled. One week went by, two weeks, three weeks without any word from her. Now was the time for our pastor to prove to us that he believed what he preached. Richard went about with his caged animal look. But he never doubted for a moment that he had done the right thing in letting her go.

At last the word went round — "Bintzea's back!" The whole congregation flocked to the house to see her and to hear the latest news. She had returned the same way as she had left, sitting on the roof of a train for several days. But she had achieved what she wanted. She had brought help and comfort to her brethren in need. Characteristically, she made light of her journey, and never even mentioned her personal hardship.

All this time our community was steadily growing. When we moved back to our pre-war premises in Olteni Street, all kinds of people came to the services — not only Jews, but also Lutherans, Baptists, Pentecostalists, and several from an Evangelical movement within the Orthodox Church known as the Army of the Lord.

The Mission was now officially under the care of the Norwegian Mission to the Jews. Pastor Solheim moved to Bucharest from Galatz to take charge, and this was the beginning of a fruitful partnership between him and Richard, which was to lead to many exciting new projects. They shared the preaching between them, giving the sermons on alternate Sundays. While Solheim had more to give to us believers, Richard preached more for the unbelievers. But as time passed, his sermons developed a depth and seriousness which left none of his hearers untouched. Often they had a poetic beauty, reflecting his love of nature. What it must have meant to him later to be cut off from the world of nature for so many long years!

But what struck me most in Richard's sermons now was his ruthless condemnation of sin, any sin, including that of our new communist rulers.

Someone who heard him at that time said, "When I first heard him speak the word 'sin', I wondered how he knew I was in the crowd. When he said the word a second time, I would have liked to have left the building unobserved. But I had to stay. When he said it the third time, I knew that I had to see it cancelled."

I once asked him the secret of his power in speaking out against sin. He answered, "When I am in the pulpit I take issue with the terrible wickedness which is in myself. Only those with a thorn in their own flesh shout loudly about the pain which thorns can cause."

Bintzea, too, was a good preacher, but she never liked preaching at an open meeting. However, quite a number of men used to tiptoe into the women's meeting when she was in the middle of a sermon, and she could do nothing about that! A certain Brethren assembly wanted to hear her preach, but they could not allow a woman to speak in their assembly. So they invited her to worship with them. They sang a hymn, said a prayer, and then declared the assembly was over, adding, "We have Sister Wurmbrand with us. As the service has ended, we will just stay and listen to her." She spoke to them for an hour. Happily it was not in the assembly, so the Bible teaching about women preaching had been fully respected!

Some of us who wanted to go more deeply into matters of the Christian faith formed an academic study group under the leadership of Pastor Solheim, which used to meet in his home twice a month to study the Bible and listen to lectures. After the study we usually had a discussion over a cup of tea. Many people came to this group who did not want to identify themselves with the church and never came to the services.

I had kept my Sunday School class on all through the war, when we had had to meet in the Wurmbrands' bedroom, transformed into an improvised chapel. Now we were able to hold it at Olteni Street. As the class was at the same time as the adult service, this meant that I was unable to worship with the others, so another sister, Alice, alternated with me. When, over twenty years later, I visited Israel and met some of my former pupils, it was a wonderful experience to see that they had remained faithful to the Lord.

A new, unexpected field of mission opened up. One of our sisters, Margit, had somehow got access to a women's prison, and she used to visit there regularly, taking food, medicine, Bibles and Christian literature. Many of the prisoners became interested, and some were converted. When Richard heard about this new opportunity for witness, he exhorted us to pray that the Lord would open ways to start a greater work in the prisons; he himself was the keenest in praying for this. Of course, he was thinking that he might go to the prisons as a ministering pastor, but the Lord had His own way of answering this prayer. During Richard's fourteen years in prison, he was such a blessing to most of those he came into contact with that it cannot be measured in human terms.

Now, whenever I agree with some of my friends to pray for something special, I always warn them — it is dangerous to pray if you are not willing to take the consequences. The Lord might answer your prayers in the way you least expect!

All the activity at the Mission, and especially my friendship with Bintzea and Richard, was of immense help to me when my marriage began to go to pieces. To my sorrow, my husband had become an active communist, travelling all over the country giving political lectures. He was never at home. I hardly ever knew where he was, and lived in constant terror that something awful would happen to him. The populace did not like the communists and beat them up as often as they had an opportunity. In the end, we agreed to divorce, and we parted as friends. I could never accept his political allegiance.

On the 9th of May 1945, at twelve o'clock precisely, I had stood in the courtyard where the Wurmbrands lived, listening to the peace bells. I have since seen pictures of other countries when peace came, showing the people in a frenzy of joy. As I listened to the bells, I thought how very different the issue of the war had been for us than for others in Europe. We had hoped for freedom in all its forms. But we had not found freedom from fear. As a Jewess, I had been a pariah under the Nazi regime; now it seemed that I was to be a pariah again, being opposed to communism.

There was joy in knowing that the slaughter had come to an end, but at the same time I knew a deep sadness. Would Rumania ever get rid of all the Russian troops who had occupied us and taken over power in the country? Officially we were not yet a communist state, but we could see clearly which way the trend was going. Anna Pauker, who during the war had been exchanged with a high-ranking Rumanian officer, a prisoner of the Russians, was now the leading personality in the government. Mass pro-communist demonstrations were organised by the authorities, during which time the shops were closed. I talked to some small shopkeepers. They could not refuse to close, for fear of being put on the black list.

That autumn, the communists staged a little drama in Bucharest. During one of the demonstrations there was shooting in front of the Royal Palace, and a few people were hurt and one was killed. The communists had engineered this so as to put the blame on the members of the democratic parties, most of whom were subsequently imprisoned or deported. Since we were soon to have an election, it was necessary to have a scapegoat.

When the election came, there were two main groups — the communists, disguised under an attractive name, and their right-wing opponents. For the first time in the history of Rumania women could go to the polls. I did not vote. There was a certain amount of danger in not doing so, as legitimation papers were stamped at the polling office. Anyone who did not vote was regarded as an enemy of the state. When an acquaintance reproved me for not having done my 'duty', I replied that I had nobody to vote for. How could I give my vote to either of these two parties? The communists hated God. Their opponents had the support of those who hated Jews.

The symbol of the communists was a sun, that of the opposition an eye. All the posters depicted the sun burning out the eye. Which it did. When the voting papers were counted, the communists emerged with a vast majority. That some people had been paid for voting twice, or even several times, for the communists, nobody even mentioned. The elections had been a fraud.

My thoughts began to turn to the possibility of leaving Rumania. Perhaps I could go to Norway. Or maybe Palestine? Jacob and I had often discussed, in the early days of our marriage, whether we might emigrate to Palestine when peace came. Certainly, large numbers of Jews were now doing so. But without Jacob the prospect was not quite so attractive, and besides I still had family ties in Rumania.

One Sunday morning in March 1946, the door bell rang as I was getting ready for church. A strange young man stood there. He looked embarrassed.

"Mrs. Moise? I have a message for you. Your father — "

I experienced an awful foreboding, and began to tremble.

"Is he dead?"

"He is very ill."

I could see from his manner that he was not telling the truth. When I insisted, he told me gently that my father had died during the night.

Only the day before, I had received a letter from him — full of love, as all his letters to me were — and now he was no more.

It was a terrible blow. He had been to stay with me a few

weeks before, and when he had left for Galatz he had told me how much he had enjoyed his visit to Bucharest. I remembered vividly so many things about him — his warm hands as I walked beside him as a child; his loving words to me; and all the wonderful breakfasts we had had together. We two were early risers, and whilst the others were still asleep we would feast together. He would fry fish or bacon and eggs when we could afford such luxury, and we usually drank a six-pint kettle of tea between us. In the summer we would sit out in the court-yard. My father was a great lover of flowers, something I have inherited from him, and we would enjoy their scent on the fresh morning air. We would sit there often without saying a word. It was enough for each to know that the other was present. In the autumn, he would bring home a huge watermelon, one of his favourite fruits, which was put in the cellar for several days to be cooled.

Father had loved children, and adored his granddaughter. Lisa's first word was *zeida*, Yiddish for grandfather. Now we had lost a dearly loved friend, and it was Lisa and myself who missed him most. Lisa found some snowdrops and put them in his hands for his burial. He had died quite alone in the house. Rachel had been away visiting Haim. Lisa was at the Mission. When the neighbours noticed that he had not come out at the usual time, they forced open the door and found him dead. It was his heart that had given way. When I saw him, his mouth was distorted as if in great pain, though the doctor comforted me by telling me that he had only had a brief moment of suffering.

I try to forget seeing him this way, and prefer to remember how when I was a child and sick he would sit by my bedside, singing to me in Yiddish in his beautiful warm baritone. I never hear *Mein Yiddishe Mamma* without experiencing a pang in my heart. This was the song he always sang for me.

8

Preparing to Leave

NOW THERE WAS NOTHING special to tie us to Rumania. We all
wanted to leave. Haim had married again, a very nice girl, and
they planned to make a new start in the free world. I dreamed
of going back to Norway.

One day when I was giving Pastor Solheim an English
lesson, he told me that Norway had invited six hundred Jews
from refugee camps, as a gesture to replace the Jews who had
been killed by the Germans during the war. Suddenly I saw
this as the fulfilment of my dreams. I wrote at once to Sven
Wiig and asked him to help me. Things began to happen. He
wrote that he had put in an application for me, and had received the necessary permission for me to enter the country.

But when I applied for a passport, I did not know what I was
in for. There were endless forms to fill in, stating such things as
how many languages I knew, and how often I had been abroad.
I received frequent visits from the police, on the pretext that
they needed more information.

I began to grow nervous about these visits. Fortunately I had
some very good neighbours. Whenever anybody came to visit
us — by that time Rachel and Lisa had come to live with
me — they had to pass my neighbours' door. While the husband

delayed the police, who wanted to know which was my room, the wife would slip in and warn me to lock the door. One day a friend of Rachel's was visiting us with her two-year-old son. We were stiff with fright in case he should make a noise while the police were knocking on the door.

The investigation dragged on for more than a year, and in the end I received a refusal. I sent in a new application. I was even more anxious to get out. Haim and his wife were about to leave. And then there was Lisa. What sort of a childhood was she having? During the war, she had had to go round with a yellow star on her coat, the stigma of a Jew, when she was still little more than a toddler. Now she was coming home from school with stories of how kind and good 'Papa Stalin' was. Rachel and I would look at each other in despair, seeing how our child was being poisoned. We gave her an antidote at home, a very strong one, and she was also very fond of Sunday School, where she learned something different. But it was not easy. We had to be careful what we talked about in her presence, in case her teacher should question her. Lisa was only ten, and I have never met a child more loyal than she, but we were still afraid.

Rachel did not have papers allowing her to stay in Bucharest. Whenever she went out, my heart stood still until I saw her indoors once more. One day she told me she had been invited to a wedding. When she did not come home at the time we had agreed, I was very worried, and as the night wore on my anxiety grew. I was just about to start making inquiries at the police station and the mortuary, when she made her appearance. I was so relieved to see her that I started to cry. This might seem a trifle, but in those days there were daily *razzias* in the city, when the police would seal off a certain quarter, posting officers with two or three armed soldiers on every corner, to examine people's papers. If you did not have the right papers, things could be very difficult for you and for those who were sheltering you.

To add to all this misery, there was the continuing famine. The situation had been growing steadily worse. The harvest had failed again. It was rare ever to feel wholly satisfied after a meal. There were always large queues in front of the food shops. You took your place in the queue first, and then asked what you were queueing for. There was rapidly rising inflation, which ended in the summer of 1947 with disaster for many people when the Rumanian *leu* was stabilised.

I was again giving English lessons to earn a living, but few people had money to spare for such luxuries. Some paid in kind. I would get a meal in return for a lesson. Often there would be a cup of tea, with sometimes two sugar lumps as an extra treat. I always found a way to save the sugar lumps for a more urgent occasion, or to give them to someone who needed them more than I did. Thousands of people were literally starving, and some truly terrible things happened. There had even been one gruesome case of cannibalism.

We grown-ups could bear the hunger, but when Lisa complained, "Mummy, I'm hungry," and we had nothing to give her, my heart bled. Our neighbours had three children, and we knew they were even worse off than we were.

Somehow, we managed. Uncle Milo and Aunt Fanny in America sent us parcels of food and clothing, as well as money. When the postman saw how happy we were when we got a letter from America, he began stealing the money from the letters, so we had to make arrangements for it to be sent through a bank. This was a very complicated business, and when we left the country we had to borrow money from Pastor Solheim to pay our guides across the frontier. We arranged for the bank to refund him the money from a sum of a hundred dollars we were shortly expecting from America, but he never received it.

I took time off that summer to help out at an inter-denominational camp which Richard had arranged in Predeal, with funds provided by the World Council of Churches. He got together with pastors and priests from many other churches to rent a large villa, where they ran relays of fortnightly house-parties with daily prayers and Bible studies, and excursions during the day. This kind of holiday, though a commonplace in the West, was a novelty in Rumania in those days, and made a welcome break for those who took part. In spite of the famine, the organisers had managed to provide plenty to eat. Many were surprised to find that so many people from different denominations could have fellowship together. During the war the Orthodox had fiercely persecuted the Protestants — Baptists, Pentecostalists, Brethren and Adventists. Now they ate at the same table and were at peace with everybody. I took Lisa with me, and she enjoyed playing with Mihai and the other children. For us helpers, it was hard work, but very worth while.

While I was there, Haim and his wife were due to pass through Predeal on the first stage of their journey to Palestine. I went to see them at the railway station at the appointed time, and waited for hours, but I missed them. I was not to see them again for nearly twenty years.

On my return home I made a new attempt to get a passport, and again I was refused. I came to the conclusion that the only thing to do was to leave the country illegally.

What finally decided me was an incident which started off trivially enough. I was standing in a queue for vegetables when two people in front of me started to quarrel. A fight developed, and I tried to leave the queue. The guard who was keeping the queue in order misunderstood my action and arrested me. Fortunately, many of the people in the queue knew me, and were so angry that they went along with us to the police station, where they made a ring round me and, while they were arguing with the guard, let me escape.

I dared not go straight home in case anyone was following me, and when I at last reached the house I was shaking so much that I went into my neighbour's flat to recover. I did not want to tell Rachel what had happened, but she saw at once there was something wrong. Later, talking the incident over, we agreed that the best thing would be to try to get out as soon as possible, before the situation grew even worse. The people who had defended me had shouted at the guard, "We had to put up with the Nazi terror for four years. Now you communists are even worse." At least the Nazis didn't arrest a defenceless woman for leaving a queue! We had an idea of what was coming, and wanted Lisa to grow up in a free and democratic country. So I started to look for a man who could guide us over the frontier.

Finding a guide proved to be more difficult than I had thought. Though I knew many Jews were leaving the country in the company of a leader from Bucharest, I was unable to discover who was organising it. We were now well into September, and I was afraid that if we did not leave soon, winter would set in and flight would be impossible. I put it to Rachel that we should leave the city and try to find a leader in one of the frontier towns.

Rachel was not keen.

"We might as well wait till the spring, now," she suggested. "Surely things can't get much worse. We don't want to find ourselves destitute in a foreign country in the middle of winter."

I did not agree.

"If we wait for the spring, it will be too late. We'll never get out."

I was proved right. Three weeks after we left, the frontiers were closed.

While we were making our preparations, Richard was once again arrested. This time we were seriously alarmed, as the communists had sworn that they would destroy him when they could get at him. We knew where he was being held, but nobody was allowed to visit him. Bintzea continued with her work as usual, trying to comfort and encourage others — she who needed so much comfort herself! But when I was alone with her she did not try to hide her anguish, and for the first time I saw her cry. One day I was just about to leave her when a very trying visitor called. Bintzea's eyes filled with tears. "Please don't leave me now," she begged. I had never seen her in such a state.

Rachel and I had started quietly selling our things. I had collected quite a good library, and selling my books was the hardest undertaking. I found a solution. I made a present to my most intimate friends of the books I was most fond of.

We decided to leave on the 21st of October, and on our last Sunday in Bucharest half the community had their dinner in the Wurmbrand home. For the last time I performed my usual duty of helping Bintzea serve the meal. Optimistically I announced, "Two weeks from today I shall be having my dinner in Oslo!"

Two days before our departure, Richard reappeared. The authorities had had no real complaint against him, and had let him go, reserving to themselves for later the right and pleasure to rearrest him. For the time being they wanted to find out, by keeping watch on him, who his associates were. He looked haggard and miserable, as if he had come back from the grave. That only three weeks in prison could change a man so completely, I would not have believed had I not seen it with my own eyes. He was ill and coughing badly. Bintzea put him to bed and nursed him lovingly, her face radiant with happiness at having got her Richard back — the more so because one of the examining officers had not only been converted, but had even shown him the denunciations which had caused his arrest. In this gesture, Richard saw a sign of genuine repentance.

I, too, was happy. Knowing that he was a free man again, it was easier for me to leave my friends. As I kissed him goodbye, I asked him if he had any message for the *Israelmisjonen* in Norway.

"Tell them that the earth is burning under our feet," he said.

I begged him to reconsider the idea of leaving the country, as it was clear to all of us that he and his family were in great danger.

He gave such a definite 'No,' that there was no point in arguing with him.

He tells me now, that I then and there promised to do

everything in my power to get them to Norway. I cannot remember doing this, but I am very grateful and even proud that the Lord eventually used me to bring these dear friends of mine out into the free world, where they have been of such great blessing to so many.

9

Escape to the West

"WHAT NAME DID YOU say, madam?"

I stood at the reception desk of one of Copenhagen's most elegant hotels, conscious of my mouldy fur coat and the none-too-clean handkerchief which covered my hair. Beside me, Lisa, tired and dishevelled, was standing guard over our two battered suitcases, held together with string. The clerk, who was regarding me with thinly disguised consternation, repeated his question.

"Moise," I said firmly. "I understand Mr. Wiig has booked us a room."

The clerk recovered his poise. "Yes, madam, of course. The porter will show you the way."

It was a dream of a room, all done out in blue and beige. I have never felt more out of place anywhere in my life. I had a bath and washed my hair. It was marvellous, but it didn't get rid of the lice.

That fur coat! How many times in the last few months I had nearly thrown it away in desperation! I had worn it in the first place because it was the warmest thing I had. When we set out on foot that moonless night in early November to follow an unknown guide into Hungary, I was wearing two dresses, two skirts, several sets of underwear — and the fur coat. We had waited ten days in the frontier town of Satu Maru before we had found two men to guide us, and now there we were, a small party of us, Rachel, Lisa and myself, another young family with two small children aged four and six, a Catholic priest and the two dubious-looking guides.

The children had been given a sleeping draught, and the men took turns in carrying them. Lisa walked with us. We passed through sleeping villages, where the dogs raised a mad barking until it seemed certain that someone would be roused and discover us. Once I saw the silhouette of a soldier, standing in a lighted doorway and calling to his dog. My heart lurched and I went literally stiff with fright. However, the wind was blowing the other way so the animal did not hear or smell us, and the soldier soon disappeared into the house.

We walked through woods, through villages, through ploughed fields. We walked the whole night through until I felt as though I had wheels in my hips which kept my legs moving automatically. I wondered if I would ever be able to stop. I looked at Lisa, plodding along beside me with never a word of complaint. My heart went out to her. At only ten years old she had already experienced so much hardship and want. But she had also learned the love and joy of friendship, so I knew that whatever life had in store for her, she would stand on solid ground.

It was seven o'clock in the morning when we reached our first resting-place. I have never seen such a filthy cottage. To reach the family quarters we had first to pass the stable where a cow and several pigs were installed. The smell was terrific.

The room where five people lived was extremely small and the furniture consisted of three benches along the walls and a table in the middle of the room. Father, mother and the eldest child each lay on a bench, while two boys were curled up in the straw on the ground. The moment we entered the room, our children threw themselves on the floor and fell asleep. We grown-ups were not allowed to sit down and were not given so much as a glass of water until we had handed over soap, sugar and other things as payment for being allowed to stay in the cottage until dark.

That night our guides took us to a Jewish family who would put us in touch with a Hungarian Jewish organisation. Their task was now ended. We paid them and thanked them for their help. They had been honest with us, and even helped us with our luggage. We had heard stories of other leaders who had first robbed the refugees and then denounced them to the police.

The next day a man with a cart agreed to take us to Pecs. Hour after hour we drove over the Hungarian plain. Though Rachel was wearing a shawl over her head, her naturally black hair turned completely grey with the dust. Whenever we saw a cyclist, another cart or even somebody walking we dared not breathe till they had passed.

At long last we arrived at Pecs, the gathering place for all refugees, where we were taken into the care of the *Alliah*, the Jewish organisation which would see us through to Vienna. That evening we were all put into a sealed cattle wagon and told to keep quiet until we got to Budapest, where we were expected by their people. The camp in Budapest turned out to be so cramped and dirty that I at once went to the Norwegian mission, where Pastor Seland greeted us with open arms and put us up for a whole week before the *Alliah* sent us on to Vienna.

That last stage of the journey was the greatest physical ordeal I have ever had to experience. There were 180 of us, packed into four lorries, so close together that I could not even raise a hand to my mouth to take a bite of the loaf of bread we had each been given by way of rations. When the children wanted to relieve themselves they had to do it over the tail-board of the lorry. Some were too nervous, and later wet their parents' laps. We dared not stop to let them get out.

Suddenly a murmur of anguish passed through the lorry. For some time we had seen a private car driving behind us. Now a second car arrived and drove in front of the first lorry. We all thought, "This is the police, and we are done for." It was the police, but they had merely come to see us safely to the Austrian frontier. The *Alliah* had paid a certain sum per head for each refugee to the Hungarian government, and it was in their interest to know that we had crossed safely into Austria.

In the middle of a forest the lorries were stopped and we all got out, to have some food and a rest before we started walking. It was raining heavily. The mud stuck to our feet, so that each step became an effort. My fur coat, soaked through, became heavier with every step. Gradually I threw away most of my luggage, including a blanket, which I was to regret later.

Rachel and I, our nerves on edge, started bickering. At one point I lost sight of her in the dark, and unthinkingly called out her name, at which a man walking behind me slapped me so roughly that I fell. We were passing through the Russian-occupied zone, and I might have betrayed the whole party. There was another moment of panic later in the night, when we thought we had lost Lisa.

Rachel had insisted on bringing too much luggage. I had warned her that she could not expect me to help her. But when I saw her staggering under the load and sobbing, I reached out to lend her a hand with her suitcase. All at once I clearly sensed the presence of my father, and heard his voice saying, "I will help you, my children." At that moment it felt as if the suitcase had been taken out of our hands. I looked at Rachel: her step had become buoyant, her breathing was regular, and there was a new light in her eyes. A hush came over us. A little later, an Austrian soldier approached us, seemingly from nowhere. I was sure we were about to be arrested, but instead he asked us politely if he could help with our luggage.

It was not until some months later that I dared to say to Rachel, "You know Daddy came to help us that night we crossed over into Austria."

She looked at me in amazement. "Did you feel it too? I didn't like to say anything to you because I was afraid you might laugh at me."

The refugee camp to which we were taken in Vienna was a former school with large rooms, each of which served twenty-five of us as bedroom, living room and kitchen. The dirt and misery were indescribable. Though I have never been particularly fussy about food, for six weeks I could hardly touch a thing. The taste was not too bad, but everything we were given was a yellowish-green colour, which took away my appetite before I started eating. Before going to the lavatory we had to put on rubber shoes, but even these did not always help. However, in spite of all these privations, I was happy. We were at last in a free country.

The camp was Jewish, and I knew that if they discovered I was a Christian I might be in difficulties. So I read my Bible secretly, but after six weeks somebody betrayed me — I discovered later it was someone who had lived next door to the Wurmbrands and recognised me as a friend of theirs. I was summoned to the camp authorities, who accused me of being a traitor to my people, and turned me out. Rachel and Lisa were expelled with me.

We were given temporary refuge by some Catholic nuns who ran a shelter for prostitutes, until we could find further accommodation — no easy task. An 'Aryan' camp refused to take us because we were Jews. At last, thanks to the help of a lady from the Norwegian Red Cross, we were readmitted to the original camp, where for a long time we were ostracised by the other inmates.

For all that, life in the camp did have its brighter moments. On the 21st of November 1947, the day it was announced that the Jews were to have a national home in Palestine, the whole camp burst into wild rejoicing. We feasted off a special ration of fried chicken and white bread, and there were chocolates and extra milk for the children. Late into the night we sang Jewish songs, danced and made music. Temporarily forgetting our difficulties, we joyfully embraced one another and thanked God that we had lived to see this moment.

Twenty years later, I experienced another of the great

moments in the history of the Jewish people. I was in Israel when Jerusalem was liberated on the 7th of June 1967. I can honestly say that, next to my baptism, that was the greatest day of my life. For the first time I fully understood how close the city of Jerusalem is to the heart of every Jew — old or young, rich or poor, intellectual or uneducated — wherever he lives on the surface of the earth. "If I forget thee, O Jerusalem, let my right hand forget her cunning."

I stayed in the camp for three months before I received a Norwegian passport for Lisa and myself. Rachel, who wanted to go to Israel, had to remain behind. Though Lisa was sad to leave her mother, she was looking forward to the train journey; she had heard that there would actually be a sleeper, with clean sheets!

And so we got to Copenhagen. And the next day Oslo, where Sven was waiting for us on the quayside. As I watched the coastline of Norway come into view through the cold and fog, I wondered what the future would bring. Paul's words came into my mind: "Forgetting those things which are behind, and reaching forth unto those things which are before", and I resolved to try to be a good citizen of my adopted country.

10

Norwegian Citizen

IT WAS NOT easy to make a new start. First, I had to go into hospital for an operation. When I was fit again, I took work as a housemaid, and went to secretarial classes in the evenings. After a year I had an office job with quite a good salary, and had found a tiny bed-sitter and kitchenette where I could make a home for Lisa; she had been staying with friends until I was settled. We have a saying in Rumania, "*Sarut mana* — kiss your hand", which we use when we want to thank someone in a special way. One day when Lisa had scrubbed the floor, I said to her, "*Sarut mana*," and she answered, "It is I who should say *sarut mana*, because if it were not for you I would not have any floor to scrub." So grateful we were to have a small home together.

Not long after my arrival in Norway, I recieved a short note from Bintzea, saying, "Richard is ill and in the sanatorium," from which I knew that he was in prison again. Poor Bintzea and Richard! My heart went out to her, knowing well how much they would have to suffer. I knew, probably better than anyone else, how much she adored Richard, and how he depended on her. But she would never show her despair.

Now that I had a little money of my own, I could begin to

think of ways of helping my friends in Rumania. Out of my tithe I started sending an occasional parcel, and so there began in a small way a work I have carried on for more than twenty years. I do not know how many parcels I have sent, nor exactly how much money has passed through my hands for this work. But I think it is not improbable that at least £30,000 has been given to me by private persons and various organisations to send help to Christians behind the iron curtain. I have since met some of those who received parcels, and they have told me that it is only due to this help that they were able to survive. Most of the recipients were so poor that they could not keep the contents for themselves, but sold them and used the money to buy food and other vital necessities. I was touched to get a letter from my friend Riva, saying, "I am happy to tell you that at last I have been able to buy a broom and a saucepan, which I have badly needed for many years."

Though I soon made many good friends in Norway, I found I pined for the fellowship of Hebrew Christians. It was the Jewishness I missed. Those few whom I had met since coming to Norway had allowed themselves to become totally assimilated; it seemed that from the moment they had been baptised they had almost forgotten that they had ever been Jews. This is something I have never been able to understand. For myself, becoming a Christian has meant that I have wanted to become an even better Jewess than I was before. After all, Jesus Christ is a Jew, and He is my Elder Brother.

So my starved Jewish *neshoma,* my soul, came alive again when I attended a Scandinavian Hebrew Christian conference in Göteborg, sponsored by the International Hebrew Christian Alliance. Shortly after my return home I was appointed representative for Norway and the year after I was co-opted as a member of the Executive Committee of the I.H.C.A. I was able to persuade the other members of the committee to allow me a larger yearly sum to be used for the Hebrew Christians in Rumania, and from now on I was able to send parcels regularly to those who were in need.

In 1948 Herzi and Pastor Solheim and his family had to return from Rumania. Poor Herzi was nearly eighty, and had hoped to spend the rest of her life with her 'children' in the country she had grown to love. The next year Mami was expelled. She brought the bad news that Bintzea too was now in prison, and Mihai was being cared for by one of the sisters. I collected the best clothes I had – clothing was still rationed in Norway – including my good winter coat, from which we made a kind of boiler suit to keep her warm when she was working on the infamous canal. Of course, these things never reached her.

There seemed so little that I could do. With both Richard and Bintzea in prison, and no means of getting in touch with them, nor even of knowing whether they were dead or alive, all I could do was pray, and continue whenever I could to send a little material help to others who, though they were not imprisoned, were suffering almost as much.

There were those who tried to dissuade me. "You are not very well off yourself," they argued. "Why deprive yourself still further, when you can't be sure that the help you send will even reach those who need it? It's only a drop in the ocean."

To which I always replied that, as long as we can do no more, it is our duty to hand out even that small drop. We must be faithful in the small things. Then the big things will come by themselves.

I became a Norwegian citizen. On the 27th of March 1953, I swore allegiance to the Norwegian constitution. It was wonderful to feel I belonged somewhere; that I now had all the rights and duties of the other inhabitants of this beautiful and friendly country; that I had become one of them. I had never really felt that I belonged to Rumania. That country had caused me too much suffering. My nightmares were becoming less frequent, but to this day I still sometimes have a dream that I am walking down a street in Bucharest where arrests are going on and I am among the victims. It was not until some years after I came to Norway that I could catch sight of a policeman without my heart standing still. I was once alone in the office when two men in uniform walked into the room. I nearly fainted. The poor men had only come to inspect the fire alarm!

The ill health that had troubled me all my life began to plague me again and I had to spend more long spells in hospital. In the autumn of 1954 I underwent a spine graft, and spent months in a plaster cast which covered most of my body. Lisa had long since gone to Israel, to live with her mother, who had married again. Mami, too, was in Israel. Herzi was living in the country. So I had none of my dear ones near me at this time, though people were very kind. Once a week a woman came to clean my flat; a friend who is a nurse came every few days to wash me under the plaster, and my friends across the street, Blanchi and Gyuri, visited me as often as possible, and helped me with the shopping.

I was off work for thirteen months in all. At that time the Norwegian health service was not as well developed as it is now, so that for six months I had an income of only about six pounds a month. I learned to make small plastic animals, and flowers out of beads, which I sold to bring in a little extra money. It was not easy, as I was unable to sit upright; the plaster kept me in a permanent half-lying posture. I read a lot, and started a correspondence course in French. But writing was too difficult and I had to give it up. I seemed doomed never to learn French properly!

Getting the plaster off was not pure pleasure. I had forgotten how to sit up, and my muscles had to learn all over again. Walking required great care. When I went back to work, it had to be only part time. However, little by little I grew stronger, and I was indescribably grateful to have the normal use of my arms and legs once more.

I was now keener than ever to help my friends in Rumania, especially when news came that Bintzea was out of prison. She wrote seldom, and her letters were always carefully worded, but at least I knew that she was alive. Nobody knew anything of Richard. Afterwards we learned that this was because he had been given a false name on the prison records so that nobody could trace him. I remembered how fervently he had prayed for Christian work in prisons. Now he was himself the answer to his prayer. I, too, prayed — that he might be a great blessing to all with whom he came in contact. This prayer also was answered in the most wonderful way.

Then one day in 1956, I received the astounding news that Richard, whom most had given up for dead, had been freed after eight years of detention. The story was that he had been so ill that the authorities were afraid he would die in prison. Not wanting this to happen, they released him. News of this sort spreads quickly in Rumania, and brethren from all over the country came to see him, bringing all kinds of gifts, mostly of food. Good care and plenty to eat were the very things he needed, and in a short while he had picked up so well that he started preaching again. A mutual friend of ours, who had been baptised by Richard in prison, visited Norway about this time, and he told me something which touched me immensely, but did not surprise me, knowing Richard as I do. It seems the government offered Richard money if he would stop preaching. To which Richard answered, shortly and concisely, "Freely I have received the Gospel, freely I give it."

Within the Hebrew Christian congregation, however, it seemed that things were far from happy. After Richard had been arrested and Solheim left Rumania, the church had been left in the care of two young men: David, whom Richard had helped with his theological training, and Peter, a young German Jew who looked on himself more as a German than as a Jew or a Rumanian. Peter was something of a highbrow; he was said to 'preach to the giraffes'. He tended to have a cold nature, which did not endear him to the people. Neither David nor Peter were born leaders. Moreover, the people keenly felt the loss of Richard and Bintzea. So the congregation gradually dwindled.

When Richard returned, of course they came flocking back. This was a cause of jealousy, and David and Peter, who considered themselves the rightful pastors, forbade Richard to preach. Richard and Bintzea found that all sorts of small difficulties were put in their way. To add to the tension, they were sharing a flat with David and Mary, and quarrels developed, one of which ended in Mary slapping Bintzea in the face. David wrote me letters full of complaints about Richard, while Richard wrote sadly that "the child whom I have nurtured at my breast has given me much pain." This was the strongest expression he ever used about the situation. When he was arrested again after two years of 'freedom', David sent me a triumphant letter, ending with, "This man is now rotting in prison."

It was all very sad. People who were in Rumania at the time have since told me that it was David himself who denounced Richard and thus brought about his rearrest and his second term of imprisonment. Richard himself has told me the full story, but he will never make it public. I have never heard him speak in any other way than lovingly about those who informed on him, and he has forbidden anyone else to speak of them harshly, though he himself is very harsh towards those who inform against others. When asked about his denouncer, Richard just shrugs his shoulders, and his answer invariably is, "He has done me no harm. No man can hurt me who does not make me wicked like himself. It is those who do evil who suffer from it."

So Bintzea found herself once more alone, with no other means of existence than the parcels she received from her family and from me. But, knowing her so well, I knew she would go hungry and give away her last slice of bread if she thought that someone else needed it more. When I heard that she had begun knitting to earn some money, I was thunderstruck. In all the years I had known her I had never seen her with a piece of knitting or sewing in her hands. She found such occupations terribly boring, and considered them a waste of time which could be put to better use — like reading, or visiting the sick and needy.

So far as I understood from her letters, which were mostly written in a kind of code, she did not want to leave Rumania as long as Richard was in prison, though she had been told officially that he was dead — which she did not believe.

I was therefore greatly surprised after a time to receive a letter asking me to try to get her and Mihai out. Mihai was due to do his military service, and they wanted to avoid his serving in a communist army. He had been having great difficulties with his studies. He had begun by studying medicine, but was expelled as soon as the authorities discovered that his father was a political prisoner. Then he went to the polytechnic, where the same thing happened. He tried again with theological studies, this time in another town, but again he was expelled.

I at once approached the Norwegian immigration office, who were most helpful. I would have to stand guarantee for Bintzea and Mihai until they were able to earn for themselves, and this, of course, I was only too pleased to do. There was no difficulty about getting their visas to enter Norway. The problems arose in Rumania, where the authorities refused to let them go. I enlisted the help of the Red Cross, who wrote to the Rumanian Red Cross, but received no answer. After we had made several attempts, Bintzea sent me a post card telling me that the Rumanians had informed her it was not in their domain to help her.

It seemed that there was nothing to be done. We put the idea away for a while, hoping that something better would crop up in due time.

II

Waiting

I NOW HAD A flat of my own — with a garden. All my life I had
longed to own a garden, and this longing was at last fulfilled.
My health had improved, and I was working full time again in
a good job. Best of all, Lisa was back with me. She had returned to Norway to train as a nurse. I had missed her terribly
all these years. Now it seemed that the sunshine was brighter
and the flowers more colourful because she was near me. Of
course, she had to live in at the hospital, but she came to see me
whenever she was off duty. We had always been very close, and
now that she was grown up she became more of a friend than a
niece.

My life ought to have been completely satisfying. I had a
good job, my own flat, and one of my family with me. Besides
my job, I was active in the church with Sunday School work,
Bible classes, the women's guild and other activities. As a
member of the Executive Committee of the I.H.C.A., I was
often abroad at congresses, where I met many interesting
people and made some good friends. I was also fully occupied
with the steadily increasing work of sending parcels behind the
iron curtain, and keeping in touch as much as possible with

Bintzea and other Rumanian friends. Naturally, I had a vast correspondence.

The result of all this was that suddenly my health gave way again. My stays in hospital became longer, and more frequent. I was forced to go back to part time work, which meant that there was less money, but I always had what I needed, and something to give away.

I had written to Bintzea describing my garden, with its fruit trees and berries. Now, in nearly every letter, she included a sentence: "I hope one day you will invite me to eat the fruits of your garden." I was puzzled why she should repeat this so often. Then suddenly, in the middle of the night, it came to me. I woke with a start. Of course, she wanted me to make a fresh attempt to get her and Mihai out. And this time, I would try to get Richard out too.

The very next day I put in an application for the three visas. But Richard was still in prison. We had heard that he was alive — in a very bad state, though Bintzea had somehow succeeded in smuggling food and medicine to him. I was told it was impossible to grant a visa to someone in prison. However, I persisted, explaining that we were working for Richard's release and that it would be easier to do so if he was able to quit the country as soon as he was freed.

In the end I succeeded. There was, however, a condition. All three of the Wurmbrands had to be in Norway within a year. I explained that we could not possibly guarantee this. The official was very kind. He suggested that I should let him know when everything was in order, and the visas would then be sent to them. Meanwhile, Richard remained in prison, and everything concerning the Wurmbrands was uncertain.

I cannot remember how it came to my knowledge that Richard's brothers were also trying to get him released. I had met two of his brothers, who together with their mother had left for Palestine during the war. One of them, Lazar, came to Norway in the summer of 1962 to talk things over with me.

Lazar indicated that a large sum of money would be needed to ransom the whole family. After we had discussed the matter, I arranged an interview with the president of the *Israelsmisjonen*, Mr. Rosef. The sum in question was five thousand dollars, and I therefore proposed on the spot that the *Israelsmisjonen* and the I.H.C.A. should each contribute two thousand dollars, while the family should find the remaining one thousand. Mr. Rosef contacted the other members of the committee, who readily agreed to pay the two thousand on condition that the Alliance did likewise. The Executive Secretary of the Alliance, the Rev. Harcourt Samuel, wrote expressing agreement on their part. The money was transferred to a bank in Switzerland, and the account frozen until the Wurmbrands should be out of Rumania.

At the same time we were also trying other means to bring pressure to bear on the Rumanians. My contact at the Immigration Department arranged an interview for us with a very high-ranking official at the Department for Foreign Affairs, who turned out to be kindness personified. Having listened to all the facts, he told us that there was to be a cocktail party the following evening at the Royal Palace, when the new Rumanian ambassador to Sweden, who was also accredited to Norway, was to present himself at court. He promised to tell the new ambassador that Norway would appreciate it if the first act of friendship from the Rumanian government would be the release of Richard Wurmbrand from prison, and permission for the whole family to leave Rumania.

Next morning he told me over the phone that the ambassador had been most obliging, and would like me to ring him to give more details. I telephoned the ambassador, who suggested that I should draw up a memorandum and go to Stockholm for an interview with him. By this time Lazar had returned to Israel, so I had nobody to consult. However, I considered that there was too much at stake and that it would be too risky for me to enter any Rumanian embassy. I had also been told that the chances would have been greater had I been a relative of the Wurmbrands, even a distant relative. But our relationship was purely of the spirit, and this would have no validity for governments. The end of the matter was that I neither went to Stockholm, nor did I write any memorandum. I should have had to sign it, and my name was known to the Rumanian authorities.

Richard's family remained in constant contact with me, and they also put me in touch with one of Bintzea's brothers in Paris, who was a doctor. Now Bintzea's letters constantly urged me to "do whatever the doctor tells you in order to get well". As it was known that I was in poor health, the censors' suspicions were not aroused by this plea, which I correctly interpreted as an instruction to follow her brother's advice in the matter of getting them out.

All my spare time was now occupied in writing, cabling and telephoning anyone I thought could be of any help. Thus I got in touch with many people whom I did not know personally, who promised their help, but unfortunately things were at a standstill. It caused me great distress to have to keep writing to Bintzea, "the doctor cannot help me", but I never gave up hope. Whenever I found the faintest line to follow up, I tried again.

Well-meaning friends urged me to give up tilting at windmills. Among these was a gentleman in Canada, who had taken a prayerful interest in the affair. He wrote me a kind letter, suggesting that I should save myself future disappointment and heartache by recognising defeat now. Of course, I could not take his advice. A few years later, this gentleman was lying ill, and turned on the television one evening without knowing what was on the programme. Great was his astonishment when he heard and saw Richard speaking of his experiences. He was deeply moved.

So 1962 passed, and most of 1963. Nothing happened. On the contrary, there were further setbacks. At the end of March, I heard from Richard's family that a certain Mr. X. Y., who was in charge of Richard's case and was negotiating with the

Rumanian authorities concerning the family's release, was shortly going to Bucharest and would take up the matter personally.

I was told further, "I have spoken to him on the telephone, and he assured me that he would do everything possible to obtain a favourable result. I, on my part, assured him that the money deposited would remain at the bank in Zürich, but I have not yet the heart — though the family in Paris insisted — to tell him that if he cannot obtain an exit visa for Richard, we want to get out the rest of the family, or even only Mihai. This restriction of the mandate can come later if the new efforts for the whole family are without result. On the other hand, would Bintzea go away with Mihai and leave Richard alone in prison in Rumania?"

For days after receiving this letter I was sick at heart, not having the courage to write to Bintzea.

"Have you written yet?" Lisa kept urging me, and my answer was always the same: "I daren't. I haven't the heart to disappoint her."

"But you must do it soon," Lisa protested. "You know she is waiting to hear from you."

In the end, of course, I had to write, though I dreaded the answer.

When it came, it was something quite different from what I had expected. Bintzea was actually comforting me for not having succeeded! I should have known — she understood how I must be feeling, and thought I needed encouragement.

At the end of September, I heard again from Mr. Harcourt Samuel. Another of Richard's brothers, Theodore, had called to see him, and told him the ransom money had been doubled. The family could raise another thousand dollars, but that left four thousand still to be found. However, the Alliance was prepared to double its own commitment, if the Norwegian Mission would do the same. I at once contacted the *Israelsmisjonen*, and received their promise for the remaining two thousand dollars.

It was, of course, a large sum, but I have often thought that if the Rumanians had fully realised what they were letting loose, they would not have let Richard go for ten times that amount, however desperate they were for hard cash.

It is interesting that they did not even pretend that it was anything other than a commercial transaction. I have an official letter, written by the representative of the Rumanian government for this slave trade, in which he openly gave his full name and address. It was a matter of selling human beings like cattle. The better the cattle, the higher the price.

Just at this stage my personal affairs took a turn for the worse. By the end of 1963 my arthritis became so painful that my doctor suggested a series of gold injections. I was ready to try anything; for years I had not been able to hold a needle, and Lisa had even had to do my darning and sew on my buttons. The gold helped. The pain soon grew less. But the treatment had unfortunate side effects, and I had to go into hospital for two months.

I had been back at work a few days when the managing director called me to his office. Hastily I took up my shorthand pad and went in, prepared to take dictation. But something else was afoot.

"Had you ever thought you might be better off in a different job, Mrs. Moise?"

"Why no," I answered. "I've always been very happy here."

I liked my work, and besides it would be very difficult for me to find a new job at my age. In three weeks I would be fifty.

The boss ceased to be friendly. He told me frankly, and at length, that he could no longer keep me on. I was away too much on sick leave, and they could not continue to put up with the inconvenience. I protested that I had been genuinely ill, but he remained unmoved.

"All right," I said at last, "if you want me to go, I will,

but you must give me notice in writing, and state the reason."

I did not think he would do it. But before I left that afternoon, I had the written notice in my hand. I even had to sign a receipt for it.

Life now became extremely difficult. I was unable to find another job. Prospective employers always asked about my health, and I could not lie. At last I registered with an agency for temporary work, helping out at different offices for a week here, a few days there. It was interesting, and I met a lot of pleasant people. But in the long run it was not a good solution to my problem. I found it too strenuous.

Lisa was very bitter at my plight. One morning at breakfast she suddenly clenched her fist and almost shouted, "Why did he have to let this happen to you?"

"Whom do you mean?" I asked mildly, "Mr. S., or God?"

"Him above," said Lisa.

I suggested that perhaps the Lord wanted to test me.

"I think He has already tested you enough," she protested.

"I've always loved the story of Job," I told her. "When Satan comes before God to accuse His children, God puts Job on a pedestal, and even boasts about him, like a father bragging about his favourite son. It is because God knows that Job is strong enough to bear any suffering that he lets Satan test him. And the outcome of the testing is that Job receives a double blessing."

I was afraid Lisa would laugh, but she merely said thoughtfully, "Oh, well then, if that's how you look at it, then it's O.K."

I did not get a new job, but one day when I was mowing the lawn I fell and broke three ribs, and that was the end of my career as a secretary. I applied for a pension from the health service, which I received in due time.

Now I had all the time I needed to work for the Wurmbrands. In the days before they finally arrived in Norway, I literally sat by the phone all day long. I would never have been able to do this had I had a job.

So God knows what He is doing, even when it is painful for us and we cannot understand why He should treat us so harshly.

12

Release

A SMALL PARAGRAPH IN a newspaper caught my eye one day in the early summer of 1964. The Rumanian government was to release several thousand political prisoners before the 23rd of August, the twentieth anniversary of the country's liberation from the Nazis. I wondered if Richard would be among them. I knew he was not classed as a normal political prisoner — he was considered one of the greatest enemies of communism.

In July I was in Denmark, undergoing further treatment for my arthritis. I had packed and was all ready to leave in a couple of hours, when the mail arrived. A post card from Bintzea had been forwarded to me from Oslo. It did not contain any special news. But after having signed it, she had added something on the side. I turned the card round to read it: "I have just spoken to Richard on the telephone, and he is coming home tomorrow."

For a few moments I was absolutely paralysed. Then I began to cry, loudly, the tears streaming down my face. I cried as if I could never stop again. The other guests flocked round me in concern. People came hurrying from all parts of the house to see what was happening. When at last I could master my emotion, I explained that I was crying for joy!

To my surprise, I discovered that very few of them knew of the situation of Christians behind the iron curtain. The people with whom I had contact were not interested — mostly they gave me the cold shoulder. Moreover, there was a communist couple at my table who had recently visited Rumania as members of a delegation, and had found it wonderful. They had seen no signs of poverty anywhere, and all the people enjoyed perfect liberty. I asked them where they had stayed in this paradise. They had lived at Predeal, in the former Royal Summer Palace, and had of course only met the cream of the communist party. No wonder they had seen no poverty. And not having been in touch with the common people, they could not discover what the man in the street thought about that 'perfect liberty'.

Now that Richard was out of prison, our hopes began to rise again that we would be able to get the whole family out of Rumania. The ten thousand dollars was still on deposit in the Swiss bank. The Alliance and the Norwegian Mission, having abandoned hope that the Wurmbrands would ever be able to come to the West, had wondered if it might be possible to get the money back. But I remembered the gardener in Jesus's parable, who pleaded with his master to wait to see if the fig tree would bear fruit next year, and I asked them to let the money remain in the bank for a while. At the very least, I intended that we should get some interest on it.

From now on our correspondence was more regular. I did everything Richard and Bintzea asked me to, and kept in touch with their brothers. I would suddenly receive a letter from Bintzea asking me to send three parcels by air, one for each of them. This meant that their departure was imminent. But time passed and nothing happened. In March 1965, Bintzea wrote that they were expecting to leave in six weeks' time, and again asked for three parcels by air. But April passed, May passed, June passed, and they were still in Rumania. Later, they told me that they had actually been on the list of those to whom passports had been granted, but at the last moment these had been cancelled.

When the whole summer had gone by, and autumn came and went, even I began to be discouraged. With the coming of winter, a deep depression settled over me. I was terribly worried about them. I had heard of cases when people had actually been on the plane, and had been turned off and had to return home. I hoped that this had not been the case with the Wurmbrands.

On the 6th of December, I woke with a splitting headache and feeling more than usually depressed. At noon the door bell rang. There was a telegram. Usually I get my telegrams over the phone, so I don't know what happened that day. After signing the receipt, I hardly dared look at it. I began trembling all over, and had to have a rest before I had the courage to open it. It read: WE ARE LEAVING BUCHAREST THIS MORNING. RICHARD.

Suddenly it was as if my room was flooded with sunshine, and a quiet, wonderful happiness took possession of my whole being. I grabbed the phone and rang Lisa to tell her the good news. I could almost hear her smile with joy at the other end of the phone. For the rest of the day I had to take myself in hand, not daring to give full vent to my joy — still not quite sure that they had escaped. But when the next day I received another wire saying ARRIVED NAPLES, I was overwhelmed with gratitude to the Lord for having crowned this enterprise with success. After so many years of work and of trying every channel, I had achieved what I had been working for. My friends were at last out of danger.

When they arrived in Norway, Richard told me how he had been called to the police and told that a large sum of money had been paid for their exit permit, but that either Bintzea or Mihai must remain in the country, as a hostage lest Richard should speak openly about his experiences in prison. Richard flatly refused to comply with this. Either they all three left, he insisted, or they would all remain. The government, in need of hard cash, let them go.

Having reached Naples, they found themselves in further difficulties. First of all, their passports were taken from them by the Jewish organisation which had brought them out. When they had sorted out this problem, they were told they must send their passports to Belgrade, where Norway is represented, in order to get their visas. But they had no intention of sending them to another communist country. There was no disposition at the Norwegian Embassy in Rome for them to obtain their visas there. As they wanted to break their journey in Paris, to visit Bintzea's brother, they asked if it would be possible to get the necessary papers there. My contact at the Immigration Office in Oslo was wonderful in this crisis, and he helped in every possible way.

Eventually all was settled. They could come to Norway any time they wanted. I had already spoken to them several times on the telephone. Richard had not been too happy about coming to Norway; he was afraid of being a burden to the *Israelsmisjonen*, as he did not know the language. I had to use all my powers of persuasion to induce him to come, and at last he gave in.

Meanwhile he had written me a long letter of which I quote a part:

Dear Anutza

I feel a little drunk. So does Mihai. Bintzea just wants to do nothing but sleep. To have been freed from the great prison of Rumania is a bigger thing than to have been freed from a particular dungeon within that vast prison. The emotion is overwhelming.

We come from a world in which *homo homini lupus* is an insult to the wolves. Wolves simply kill their victims. The inquisitors of communism are very careful that their victims do not die, but suffer to the end. In prison, while the prisoners were forced to eat faeces and drink urine, they were kept under medical supervision. Care was taken to ensure that they had the physical strength to bear their suffering. You'll be afraid to see my body.

It is not that I have spent fourteen years in prison. 'Prison' is just a word. In my sufferings I have experienced the ultimate depths of human fierceness, brutality, perfidy and godlessness. We suffered, not so much from what they did to us — our greatest suffering was to see how bad they were, and to what extent human nature can decay. We tried desperately to see the image of God in these men. It was very difficult to discover it.

Neither those who tortured us, nor those who betrayed friendship just when they should have proved it, could do us more harm than we were able to forgive. (I say 'we', because I am expressing the feelings of the many hundreds of Christians who were in the prison. There were four hundred peasants from the Army of the Lord alone, and then innumerable priests and ministers of all confessions, Baptists, Pentecostalists, and so on.) We could do more than forgive. We could absolve.

Of all Christian thinkers, the great Reformers have helped us the most, by their teaching about the lack of free will in man. Luther said: "My Reformation stands or falls on my assertion that man has not the least amount of free will", and "The man who can abolish the words 'free will' will have done the greatest service to mankind."

You cannot reproach a crocodile for eating men. It is obeying the law of its nature. So inferior men — those to whom communism appeals consciously and whom it uses to further its aim — are simply obeying the laws of their character in being brutal and perfidious.

But we did not see only human rottenness. We have also seen the grace of God working in those horrible circumstances. I have been privileged to have as friends in prison saints and heroes of faith who are equal in stature to the martyrs of the first centuries. My time in prison has not been in vain. Prison is a parish in which it is good to work. Men have been won for Christ there. But what was more, we were weak. Our weakness made us strong. Having no power of our own, God stood by us and gave us His strength. The heavens opened for us and showed us their beauty. It would be unfair to speak of prison only as a place of suffering for Christians. It is also a place of joy which cannot be put into words.

And now we are in a free world. I have just spoken to an evangelical pastor without the fear that he will betray me to the secret police. In Rumania you are never sure of that, even if you are talking to someone you consider your best friend, even a pastor or a bishop. Only a few days ago the pastor of a little Baptist church with only twenty-two members confessed to me that he has to report regularly to the secret police with information about everything he has heard. But that is not all. He knows three members of his church who are obliged to inform on him, and so on.

We are accommodating ourselves with difficulty to our new circumstances. Everything is so strange for us.

And now, something about our situation. We escaped from Rumania with great difficulty.

First of all, they wanted to keep Bintzea or Mihai as a hostage so that I would not write against communism abroad. Then, they made it clear that if I do so, they will destroy my reputation in the Church (they have their men abroad too, even in the World Council of Churches). They told me openly, "We can easily find a gangster to kill you," and they reminded me that I can be arrested by them in the West, too. I was in prison with the Rumanian Bishop Leul whom they kidnapped in Austria.

In the end, they gave us our passports, but I am very much afraid that they have taken money from several sources. Brother Ostrowsky* told me that the Church has also had to

* A Hebrew Christian from Israel, who had visited Richard shortly after his release from prison.

pay. Why should all this money have been paid to them? If I had known, when I put in an application for a passport, that others would have to make such sacrifices for me, I would not have done it. I got the news from Brother Ostrowsky when we already had the passports.

Jews who leave the country are each allowed to take one case weighing seventy kilograms. All we owned had been confiscated when I was arrested. So we had nothing to worry about. We have only the bare necessities with us . . .

What will happen next, we don't know. The passports are retained by the Jewish Agency, which does not hand them over to the refugees, in order to oblige them to go to Israel and not anywhere else . . .

We have many problems. We talk about them, but thanks to God we do not have to worry. The God who has performed unspeakable miracles for us (in 1950 I was transferred to a cell for dying prisoners, having been abandoned by the doctors as a hopeless case) is worthy to be trusted.

But, knowing you to have been a friend in hard times, we would like to have your advice. You know the West. We have no idea of this new world.

I thank you from all my heart for all the love you have shown and continue to show us.

Those who knew you, and the many you help, asked us to give you their love.

Yours very sincerely in the Lord's service.

RICHARD

There was much more in this letter, the first Richard had written to me from this side of the iron curtain, which gave a glimpse of the terrible experiences he had been through. Bintzea also wrote:

My very beloved Anutza

I can't tell you how excited I am at the thought that we shall soon see each other again.

We are in Rome, not knowing what has been decided for us. Our 'passports' have been given to the World Council of Churches, and then we shall be able to move.

We hope then to go to Paris, to my brother's, and then after a few days to you, in Norway.

I hardly dare to write these words — the miracle the Lord has wrought for us is great. We cannot do anything else but praise Him, adore Him and thank Him.

My dear and beloved Anutza, our hearts have been refreshed by your love. In vain I would try to thank you in words. May the Lord Himself reward you greatly.

Together with Richard and Mihai I embrace you and Lisa and can hardly wait till we meet again.

It was almost Christmas. In one way, the days were flying by, as there was so much to be done. But on the other hand, when you are waiting for dearly loved friends, one of whom is part of your own soul, the minutes move at a snail's pace.

The Wurmbrands were due to arrive on the 23rd, the day before Christmas Eve. My pension had not yet fallen due, so I was rather short of money, but Lisa gave me a large sum to have a proper celebration of Christmas. She was working until twelve o'clock on Christmas Eve, so I had to do all the work. But she had given me strict orders not to decorate the Christmas tree. That she was to do herself.

When I awoke on the 23rd, it was snowing heavily, and all day long the snow fell steadily, settling on the ground and blocking streets and roads. The Wurmbrands were due to arrive at 7.30 in the evening at the international airport, but no planes could land on Fornebu that day because of the snow. I rang the airport, and heard that their plane had been very much delayed, and was being diverted to another airport some distance from Oslo. So instead I went to the air terminal in the city, and was waiting there when their bus arrived at 11.30. Every nerve in my body was tingling with excitement, and my heart was overflowing with joy. I was only sorry that Lisa could not be there. She was very fond of them, and had been Mihai's childhood playmate.

The first person off the bus was Richard. We flew into each other's arms and hugged and kissed. Mihai was the next to get off. More kisses and embraces. We were all too moved to speak. But when Bintzea stepped down I started sobbing uncontrollably. Bintzea said, soothingly, "Don't cry, Nutzule, don't cry." Her own eyes were shining with joy, and there was no trace of tears. When, much later, I asked her, "Don't you ever cry?" she answered that she dared not start weeping, or she would never be able to stop.

At the headquarters of the *Israelsmisjonen* there was a reception waiting. The table was beautifully laid, and there were sandwiches and cakes, coffee and tea. But who could eat? I was satisfied just to look at them, to feel their presence, while unspoken words of love and encouragement passed between us. It was as if a part of heaven had come down to us. My heart was nearly bursting with gratitude. I think a lark must feel like that when it soars up towards the sky, higher and higher and still higher, and then with a sudden thrilling burst of song it plunges towards its nest, as if its little heart would burst should it continue soaring upwards.

But at the same time I was sad — the suffering they had endured had left its visible marks. When Richard took off his coat, I saw a deep hole in his neck, which had not been there when I had last seen him. I asked Bintzea what it was. She only shrugged her shoulders. Later I saw all the scars on his back, his swollen legs and feet. His face was haggard, and there were deep shadows under his eyes.

I could scarcely tear myself away, but it was late. I had a very tiring day ahead of me, and they had had an exhausting journey. Arriving home, I had already begun undressing when I suddenly remembered that my Christmas tree was still in the garden — frozen. It was two o'clock in the morning, and bitterly cold. I threw my coat on, went down and had to dig out the tree from under the snow.

Next morning it was still snowing heavily, and I had the last-minute shopping to do. I had already paid for my purchases when I had a bright idea. I am not very fond of bananas, so I rarely buy any, but I thought my friends would like some. When they arrived in the afternoon, Bintzea brought a shopping bag she had bought in Paris. In it was some fruit, including some bananas! They had thought that in cold Norway we would not be able to buy exotic fruit, and wanted to give me a treat!

There followed an unforgettable evening. We talked together, sang carols and hymns, enjoyed the good food and gave thanks for our gifts. Every few minutes we broke off to hug and kiss each other. We reminisced about the old days, and they gave me news of all my old friends. But in the middle of the joy it was as though a veil had fallen over Richard's face, and his mind was far, far away.

"Richard," I said, "you are no longer in Rumania. You are in Norway, in a free and democratic country."

As quickly as it had come, the veil lifted, and he was once more with us, the life and soul of the party.

I slipped into the kitchen to prepare something to eat. Richard followed me. Suddenly he ran back into the living-room grabbed Bintzea by the hand and said, "Come, I will show you something beautiful." And he took her round the whole flat and pointed out of every window. All the houses round about were illuminated, and there were no blinds or curtains to shut off the light which was streaming out. In every house stood a Christmas tree, glowing with lighted candles.

Richard said, "Just imagine, nobody pulls any blinds or curtains here. You can look into every house and no one is afraid."

In my inner eye a picture rose up out of the past: my first Christmas, and a little boy who shouted at the top of his voice,

"I want to see the candles! I want to see the candles!"

Christmas is the time when we celebrate the coming of the Light of the world, and this same Light shines in the heart of a little boy and of a former prisoner, who suffered in order to keep that Light shining bright around him.

13

Birth of a World-wide Mission

IN JUST OVER FIVE YEARS since Richard came to the West, he has done more than most people have achieved in a lifetime. He has founded twenty-seven separate missions all over the free world, with the aim of helping Christians in communist countries. He has written seven books, which have been translated into nearly thirty languages. He frequently broadcasts on radio and television, and writes articles for journals. His public meetings usually attract thousands; crowds have to be turned away. I have often watched the faces of the audience, expressing the whole gamut of emotions — at times listening intently, or breaking into smiles or laughter, crumpled with weeping, contorted with horror; or even biting nails in agitation.

I ask myself how this man, after what he has suffered, finds the strength to do all this. Certainly, in the state he was in when he first came to the West, I would not have thought it possible.

A few days after their arrival in Norway, Richard and Bintzea were sent to a rest home in the mountains. They needed it badly. They insisted on my accompanying them, and of course I was glad to do so, though the mountains in the middle of winter are not my idea of the setting for a perfect holiday, and that winter was one of the most severe we had experienced for many years.

Richard was in a terrible state of nerves. If, while we were out walking, a car passed us, he was convinced it was the secret police. The sight of two or three people talking together in a group had the same effect on him. In vain I kept assuring him there was nothing to be afraid of. I remembered my own reactions when I had first come to Norway; and I had not suffered a fraction of what Richard had been through.

He betrayed his state of mind in many small ways. For instance, he would never tear up a piece of paper. He had been without writing paper all the years in prison. Now he treasured it so greatly that he would save every scrap.

Often, in the middle of a meal, or as we sat together in conversation, there would come over his face that strange look which I had noticed on our first evening together — a veil of unutterable sadness and despair. Bintzea would kick me under the table, and whisper, "Tell a funny story," and I would turn to him with a bright smile and ask, "Have you heard the one about . . . ?"

I racked my brains for a store of jokes over those first few days. His sense of humour astonished me. In the old days, in Rumania, he had tended to be rather puritanical and would frown disapprovingly whenever anyone made a frivolous remark. Now he would frequently roar with amusement.

I asked him some time later how this change had come about.

"You used to be so serious, I was afraid to mention anything funny. Now you are always laughing."

"Oh, that," he said. "When I was in solitary confinement I used to make a point of telling myself a new joke every day. It helped to keep me sane."

He had also preached himself a sermon every day — some of

these have since been published — and played mental chess with himself to keep his brain alert.

One of the first things I had asked Bintzea on their arrival was what had happened to Ivan and Fedora. She told me that Ivan was dead.

After having been sent to Siberia, he had been put in a labour camp, where he had to work in the forests cutting timber. It was strenuous for anybody, but more so for him, with his tuberculosis. The cold, too, was very hard to endure.

But worst of all were the interrogations. There was a woman prisoner at the camp who had been a secretary in his church. In the course of her interrogations, the secret police constantly told her she was lying, and that Ivan was saying something quite different. At last, goaded beyond endurance, she declared, "I will believe you only if I hear it from his own mouth."

So Ivan was brought before her, beaten, bloody and swollen all over his body. He was unable to stand. Nadejdia looked straight at him and asked, "Why did you say so and so?"

Ivan calmly returned her gaze and replied, simply and quietly, "Do you really think I would say that?"

He was taken away, and that was the last time she saw him.

Nadejdia served her seven years in the camp, and at the end of that time she was asked if she had now learned that God does not exist. "No," she answered, and was sentenced to another seven years in Siberia, though not in the labour camp.

Ivan remained in the camp until his death. He was a light and joy to all who met him, and never tired of witnessing for his Lord. When he felt death approaching, he called together his friends, admonished them to keep faithful, and asked them to sing something for him. They saw that he was growing weaker and weaker; then he could speak no longer. A solemn hush lay over the room. Suddenly they saw him smile, his face shining and radiant with an exceeding great happiness — then he stretched out his arms as though to embrace an unseen person, his lips moved soundlessly as if he were pronouncing a beloved name, then he fell back on his pillow. He was with the Lord whom he had served so faithfully.

As Bintzea told me his story, I could see him there before my eyes, standing firm for the Lord, and though I was crying I was happy too, praising the Lord for the privilege of having known him, and through him having been made so much richer.

The rest which the Wurmbrands so sorely needed soon turned into something different. News got around of their arrival. People who had been praying for years about starting a work behind the iron curtain, came to see Richard. Invitations to preach poured in. He left the rest home several times, and returned to Oslo after only ten days.

The meetings he addressed led to some very moving encounters. On Christmas Day he had attended the American church, at my suggestion. They had wanted to come to my church, but as they understood no Norwegian there did not seem to be much point. When they came to my home after the service, Richard was all aglow. He had introduced himself to the pastor, the Rev. Myrus Knudson, who had welcomed him warmly and asked him to come again. Later, Mr. Knudson told us that he had made a point of checking with the American authorities and the *Israelsmisjonen* to make sure that Richard was not a fake. The information proved satisfactory, so Richard was invited to preach there.

During the sermon, he noticed two ladies who spent the whole time quietly weeping. One of them, an invalid, had been praying for him for many years, and had come to church that morning not knowing who was to preach. The other lady had also had the Wurmbrands on her daily prayer list for some years. They had known that Richard was in prison. At the end of the service Richard was deeply touched to learn the cause of their tears — they had wept with joy and gratitude at seeing with their own eyes the answer to so many years of fervent prayer.

Richard's story made a special impression on the NATO

personnel in Oslo, whose pastor at that time was Colonel Sturdy. They decided that he had a most important message to bring to the world, and particularly to America, and they collected money to pay his fare to the States.

The *Israelsmisjonen* would have liked Richard to work for them in Paris, but he felt that God had trained him specially to work for the communist world. Provisionally, he agreed to go to Paris, and leave Bintzea and Mihai there while he went on a preaching tour of America. There was not enough money to send all three of them to the States.

Bintzea was in despair at this arrangement.

"Nutzule," she begged, "can't you do something to help us? You must persuade the pastor to get me a visa for the States. How can I let Richard go alone? You know how dependent he is on me, and haven't we been parted long enough?"

God works in unexpected ways. Two days before their departure, the Knudsons gave a party for the Wurmbrands. I arrived with Lisa a little late, by which time most of the guests were already present. I went round shaking hands and making myself known. A friendly-looking gentleman introduced himself as Mr. Olsson.

Laughingly I said, "Tell me, is everybody here called Olsson or Olssen? I think you are the fourth I have met this evening."

Later I found myself sitting next to him at supper. Opposite me was Pastor Knudson. Impulsively, I said to the pastor, "I want to speak to you severely."

"What have I done now?" he joked.

"It is not what you have done, it is what you have not done," I answered. I had not intended to raise the matter in front of the others, but I found myself saying, "You know Bintzea can't let Richard go alone to the States. Please, try to get her a visa, and the Lord will take care of the fare."

To my astonishment, Mr. Olsson butted in, "Bring your friend to the embassy at ten o'clock tomorrow morning, and we'll see what we can do."

"Thank you," I said, not having the faintest idea what it was all about. I wondered who Mr. Olsson was.

I arrived at the American embassy nearly half an hour early the next morning, not wanting to make Bintzea wait for me in the cold. Mr. Olsson was out, and his secretary did not seem to know who I was. When I mentioned Mrs. Wurmbrand, however, she immediately became most helpful. Bintzea arrived, and we were shown into Mr. Olsson's office. Less than an hour later, we left the embassy with the visa in Bintzea's pocket.

It turned out that Mr. Olsson was the American Military Attaché. Had I realised when I met him that he was such an important person, I might have felt shy and awkward. But he and his family were such pleasant, straightforward people, that since they have left Oslo I miss them every time I go to the American church.

The Wurmbrands left Norway after only five weeks. But before they left, the foundations of the first mission to those behind the iron curtain had already been laid.

In America, Richard preached in a great many churches, and was invited to give a lecture before a Committee of the American Senate. This caused a great storm. It was reported by the press throughout the world and raised considerable opposition from many people and organised bodies, including Christian institutions, who had not lifted a finger to help those behind the iron curtain. They maintained that by his forthright public speaking he had destroyed any chances of getting more believers out of communist countries, and that in fact he was positively endangering the position of these Christians.

However, in Rumania some of the brethren heard about this over Radio Free Europe, and their story was quite different. They were filled with gratitude that people in the West were at last being made aware of their plight. In fact, the gloomy warnings of the doubters have been proved false. Richard's organisation has since been able to ransom others from Rumania.

I was sorry when the Wurmbrands had to leave Norway so

soon. However, as it turned out, I was to see them again sooner than I had expected. They did not go at once to live permanently in America. Following Richard's tour of the States, he had a lot of requests to address meetings in Europe, so they continued to make their headquarters in Paris for some months.

In August 1966 I went on holiday to Germany, to visit my sister who was then living in Frankfurt, and Bintzea invited me to stop off in Paris on my way. Who has not dreamed of visiting Paris? I accepted with alacrity.

In fact, when I got there, I found that Richard was in London preaching, and a few days later he summoned Bintzea urgently to come and help him. The Rev. Stuart Harris of the European Christian Mission had been in Bucharest shortly after Richard's release from prison, and had visited him then. Now he had arranged a schedule for Richard to preach in Britain. Soon the second Mission to the Communist World was founded, in Britain, with Mr. Harris as Director.

I stayed on in Paris, with Mihai. Whenever he had time he took me out sightseeing, but he often had to leave me to my own devices, as he was busy studying for his degree in theology. One day I was alone in the house when the door bell rang. It was a strange gentleman, who addressed me in French. I answered in English that I was sorry I did not speak French. He then asked me what language I would prefer to speak. Thinking to put him in a spot, I said, "Let's speak Rumanian."

He did speak Rumanian. As a matter of fact, he was Rumanian-born. He had recently been back to his native country, and had there met an old friend who had told him all about the Wurmbrands and asked him to look them up when he returned. He was most disappointed to miss them, but he left a message. I was to tell Richard that in Rumania they had heard about his address to the Senate. They congratulated him for his courage, but above all they asked him to continue to tell the truth wherever and whenever he had the opportunity.

Richard has made many enemies through being so out-spoken. But he insists on telling things as they are, instead of wrapping them up in pink cellophane. It is interesting to note that most of the opposition to his work comes from lukewarm Christians and their leaders. They are afraid to believe what he tells them; they do not want to have to face up to the conse-quences. In the West we have lulled ourselves into a state of complacency with our material comforts and high living stan-dards, and we do not want to be disturbed by stories of star-vation, imprisonment, torture and persecution.

Then there are those who go about with blind eyes, not wanting to see the truth. These are people who have stayed behind the iron curtain for a week or two, or even less. They are taken there by stooges of the communists, who show them only the things they want visitors to see. They stay in the best hotels, dine at the best restaurants, and do not look about them when they are out. They do not see people standing in queues for bread and meat, twenty-five years after the war. They do not notice that the grocery shops contain little but wines and tinned foods. Do they see how badly dressed the people are? Have they seen a lady wearing a hat? Have they even seen a milliner's shop? Have they caught the fragrance of perfume from a beautiful girl passing in the street? Or even the smell of good soap? A good piece of soap is a luxury not everybody can indulge in.

But above all, when they walk along the street, have they seen anybody laugh for joy? Have they noticed how over-worked everyone looks? Do they know that the retiring age for men is sixty and for women fifty-five, but most people do not reach that age? They either die before achieving it, or have to retire many years sooner, through overwork and malnutrition. Have they been to visit the Christians in jail, or their fam-ilies?

Of course, all great men have their detractors. Dwarfs do not like giants. And Richard is a giant. But he is also human. Though he tries to ignore much of what is said and written about him, those of us who know him well can always tell when something has distressed him.

One day he was invited to be the speaker at a students' anniversary. I had been looking forward to this dinner, knowing that I would meet many old friends. At the end of the meal Richard delivered his speech, and I have never heard him so uninspired. I looked questioningly across the table at Bintzea, and her eyes telegraphed back that she would tell me later what was wrong. When we were going out after the speeches were ended, she pulled me aside and told me that Richard had that morning received a very disagreeable letter, and he had been in a bad mood all day. He had not even been able to sleep during his usual afternoon rest.

Fortunately, there are also people who know how to appreciate Richard. I have heard Bishop Nordeval, who is the president of the Norwegian mission to those behind the iron curtain, say in the course of a sermon to a packed church, that he considers Richard the greatest Christian personality of this century, and that he feels it has been a grace to have known him.

The Bishop continued: "In the work behind the iron curtain, we must stand together with Pastor Richard Wurmbrand. Pastor Wurmbrand has had to endure many disheartening examples of small-mindedness and suspicion, such things as ought to be unworthy for Christians. His is the voice of a prophet in the dark chaos of our time. I know him, and can say with frankness that there is no Christian leader in our time whom I trust more than him, because he never seeks his own, only Christ."

Bishop Nordeval himself is a giant in the Kingdom of God, so that much importance must be attached to his words.

In one of Oswald Chambers's books he writes, "Wherever there is vision, there is also a life of rectitude because the vision imparts moral incentive." I think this is a good description of Richard's life. There is a rectitude about him that not even his many enemies can slander.

A major reason for the spiritual power of both Richard and Bintzea must be the volume of prayer that goes up for them all over the world. In Russia, Christians keep a constant vigil on their behalf. At first, all these Christians knew was that a brother from another communist country, who had suffered greatly, had escaped to the West to spread word of their plight and send them Bibles and practical help. Then they learned that his name was Richard. Later they were told his full name. They decided to form a prayer rota, one church praying from six to nine o'clock, another from nine to twelve, and so on. Is it to be wondered at that, with so much prayer backing, Richard and Bintzea have outgrown most Christians? Such prayer can defeat all opposition.

I know that the opposition which caused Richard the most heartache came from those he had known in Rumania. Among these is David, who contributed to Richard's second arrest. Later he himself came to the West, and he is now a pastor in Germany. He and Mary came to Norway a few years before the Wurmbrands, having also been ransomed by the *Israelsmisjonen*. At that time I was working hard for Bintzea's release, and it pained me to hear the stories he was spreading about Richard, whom he had wronged, the more so because some people believed him, and were ready to be prejudiced against Richard from the start.

Some of this opposition to Richard has rubbed off on me, and I have had the painful experience of losing friends who had been close to me, because of my friendship with Richard and Bintzea. I have been frankly given the alternative, "Either you give up your association with the Wurmbrands, or we cannot continue to see you," and I have replied, "It is up to you. I am not breaking with you. But I don't allow anybody to choose my friends."

When we got the news that the Wurmbrands were at last coming to Norway, and I was rejoicing and looking forward to seeing them again, Lisa one day said to me, "I hope you will not be as disappointed in them as you were in Mary and David."

I answered, "I am sure I shall not be; but even if I should, it is my duty to give everybody at least one chance."

Now they have been in the free world for more than five years, I have over and over again been deeply touched to see how they show their gratitude to me. They never miss an opportunity to tell everyone they meet that, as Richard jokingly expresses it, "She is the guilty one. She is the one who worked for our release."

I was very moved to receive one day a cable which read: "This being the third anniversary of our release from Rumania express warm gratitude for everything you did for us and for the Underground Church. Thanks to you its message is now known among millions in the world. May God reward. Richard, Bintzea and Mihai."

Perhaps the true depth of our friendship is shown in a characteristic note from Richard after I had reproached him for not writing more often.

Dear Anutza
    Christ is risen.
    After His resurrection He had long talks with His disciples. To His holy mother he did not even show Himself, because she did not need it.
    This is the reason why X receives fifteen pages and you not even one. There are levels where words are useless.

The knowledge that I have friends on whom I can rely whatever happens, even though they may be far away, has been of the utmost comfort to me in moments of agony and anguish.

So, when Bintzea says to me, "May the Lord bless you for all you have done for us," I can in truth answer, "He has more than blessed me. He has showered blessings upon me ever since you entered my house."

14

Family Reunion

I STOOD ON THE tarmac at Lydda airport, breathing in the air of my ancestral home. Beyond the barrier, my family were waiting to greet me, but for a moment I was still, savouring the sensation of setting foot in the land of Abraham, Isaac and Jacob; the land where the prophets had told of a coming Messiah; where Jesus Himself had in due time been born, lived, suffered and died, had risen again from the dead and ascended into heaven, and — most important of all — to which He will return again. This moment was the fulfilment of a lifetime's ambition, born years ago when, as a child, I had witnessed the joy of the Polish *halutzim* on their way to make a new life in Palestine.

Someone called out my name. They were all there to meet me — Mami, my sister and brother-in-law, my sister-in-law and her son Norman, Lisa and a couple of other old friends. As I walked through the reception hall, I spotted my eldest nephew, Ytzhak, who had been allowed in because he was a serviceman. I treasure the memory of his sweet smile when he saw I had recognised him. When I had passed through the customs, I was instantly engulfed in a loving welcome. Nearly all of them had brought flowers, and I had to borrow some arms to help me carry the bouquets.

It was the boys who fascinated me, my brother's sons. I could not take my eyes off them, and they, too, seemed impressed by their new-old aunt. Later, when we had become good friends, Ytzhak told me, laughing, "You know, we were terrified at the thought of meeting you. Aunt Rachel had told us that you were so straitlaced that we would have to be on our best behaviour. I never thought we should come to like each other."

For my part, I adored them both. In temperament they were exact opposites. When Ytzhak came home from camp, it was as if the house was suddenly flooded with sunshine and happiness. He was forever chattering, and enjoyed life to the last drop. Norman, on the contrary, was quiet and studious. He worshipped his elder brother, and his eyes lit up with enthusiasm when Ytzhak told stories of life in camp.

I did not meet Haim until about two weeks after my arrival, as he was away from home in the merchant navy. When we did meet, it was a wonderful reunion. We had not set eyes on each other for twenty years.

I stayed in Israel for several months, and thus was there at the time of the Six Day War. In the days before the fighting broke out, we of my generation were apprehensive at the thought of a new war, while the youngsters prepared gladly to give their lives for Israel if necessary. For them it was a most spontaneous thing. Nobody thought of it as a sacrifice. It was as natural as eating or breathing to give your life at the call of love and duty. No, it was not love and duty. It was only love. And this, of course, is the reason why they won the war — they knew what they were fighting for.

That is looking at it from the human point of view. But all those I spoke to after it was over were convinced that it was God Himself who had come to the rescue of His people and given them the victory. Even the atheists looked on the issue of the Six Day War as a miracle performed by a higher power.

Ytzhak Rabin, the General of the Army Staff, spoke of it in these terms to his soldiers.

When the war finally broke out, it came as a relief. Now we knew where we stood. The days immediately preceding hostilities had been intolerable; our nerves were at the highest pitch. We kept the radio on day and night. In my sister's home, where I was living, there were incessant quarrels over which station to listen to. I favoured the B.B.C., which covered the war in an objective way — which I cannot say for it now when it comments on the Middle East situation. Lisa wanted the *Kol Israel* in Hebrew, Rachel the *Kol Israel* in Rumanian. My brother-in-law was abroad, so at least we did not have to quarrel with him.

On the 9th of June, Lisa and I were listening to the Rumanian edition, when the programme was suddenly interrupted: "Here is an important news flash: Jerusalem has been liberated."

We caught our breath and gazed at each other, our eyes filled with tears, unable to say a word. The bulletin continued with news of the liberation of Bethlehem and Jericho. This time we wept unashamedly. To think that we should live to see this moment! What does not Jerusalem mean to every Jewish and Christian heart? The Lord had said, "Jerusalem shall be trodden down . . . until the times of the Gentiles be fulfilled" (Luke 21:23). We had entered a new epoch in history.

Rachel and I went out to celebrate. The whole town was decorated with Israeli flags and bunting, all the flowers were sold out, and so were the cakes at the confectioners'. People who met in the street embraced each other, exclaiming with tears of joy, "*Baruh Hasham* — Praise the Lord!" and "*Mosel tov* — congratulations!" Complete strangers fell into each other's arms in a frenzy of jubilation. I saw only one sad face — that of a young girl. No doubt someone in her family had had to give his life.

We had to queue to buy a newspaper. Across the front page the banner headlines read, "I PRAISE THEE, LORD, KING

OF THE UNIVERSE, THAT THOU HAST ALLOWED
ME TO SEE THIS DAY", echoing the feeling of every
Jewish heart in Israel.

But the war had a sad sequel for our small family. In August,
Ytzhak was sent to England with other young men to repair and
take over a British submarine which was being sold to the Israeli navy. He did not want to leave Israel. "Supposing my
country needs me while I am away?" he said to me.

He was happy in England, however. He had seen something
more of the world, had learned to speak English fluently, and
made many new friends.

At the end of January, the *Dakar* was to return home. All
over Israel, families were preparing with feverish expectation,
mothers and wives cleaning and polishing, planning favourite
dishes for husbands and sons, counting the days.

On Saturday, the 29th of January, back in Oslo, I was listening to the morning news bulletin when it was announced that an
Israeli submarine was missing. At once I rang the news agency
to ask if it was a submarine returning from England. They said
no.

That morning I wrote to Lisa, "My heart bleeds at the news
of the missing submarine. I have one comfort, though: Ytzhak
is not on it."

I listened to every news bulletin that day, but there was no
further word of the submarine. In the evening I was looking at
the newsreel on television. Some months before, I had seen the
film *The Bible*, and had objected to the sequence where Abraham, after God had told him to sacrifice his son, runs out into
the desert, protesting, "No! No!" Surely, I had thought, no
matter what grief has befallen you, you don't behave like that.
Now, the first thing I saw on the television screen was the
Dakar in Portsmouth harbour, leaving for Israel. They said it
was still missing, with its crew of sixty-nine.

I knew then that our Ytzhak was on it. It was as if a thun-
derstorm had broken over the house; flashes of lightning
through my brain turned everything foggy and unreal, and I

began shouting wildly, "No! No!" Now I understand the Abraham in the film.

How I got through that evening I do not remember. I was quite alone in the house, and when my neighbour came in later, I asked her to come up to me. She sat with me until the small hours, unable to find anything to say. I rang my family in Haifa several times, but it was impossible to speak to them. We just cried all the time, so I was no wiser about what had happened.

Haim was at sea when he heard the news. He flew home from the first port and took part in the rescue operation. Lisa told me that they had oxygen on board for fourteen days. For the next two weeks I rang the news agency every hour, day and night, until hope was given up.

Haim's health deteriorated from the time he heard of the missing *Dakar*, and only two years later he also passed away. I have heard that many of the parents of those boys have died, or given up their businesses. They could not continue to live after their tragic loss. Alas, there is scarcely a home in Israel which has not lost at least one loved member. But life has to go on, in spite of worry. Why it has been more difficult for the parents of the boys on the *Dakar* is, I think, the sudden shock of the change from joyful expectation to desperate grief. Also, the uncertainty about what actually happened makes it harder to bear.

But though the pain of having lost two of my family in such a short space of time is constantly eating at my heart, I have not lost touch with life. I have been too busy.

I had resigned myself to the idea that, once they moved to the States, I would not see much of Richard and Bintzea. In fact, this has been far from the case. Sometimes I laughingly call myself their personal travelling ambassador.

I have grown used to getting a sudden cable, or a phone call late at night, asking me to drop everything and go to London, or Basle, or Stuttgart, to carry out an urgent errand for Richard.

I have even had the joy of visiting several countries behind the iron curtain, to take help to our suffering brethren.

Or sometimes Bintzea is alone in Europe and wants me to help her with something. She gets on the telephone to me, and we meet up in some country and work together. It is an exciting life, unpredictable, and not without its funnier moments, such as the time when they were spending a rare holiday with me in Norway, in the summer of 1968. Richard received a wire from an American senator asking him to fly over to the States to help with an anti-Vietnam demonstration. He had just time to make it before going on to Sweden, where he was to speak at several meetings. Bintzea remained with me, anxiously awaiting news. When a cable at last arrived she opened it feverishly, to read, "Sensational news. I love you. Richard."

Richard and Bintzea now spend about half the year in America, and the rest of the time travelling all over the world, addressing meetings and telling people about the needs of those in communist countries, and organising the missionary work behind the iron curtain. Whenever they are in Europe I usually join them, at least for part of the time, and travel with them. When people envy me the opportunity to see so many different countries, I have to explain that I rarely have the time to see any of the well-known places and buildings. But I do meet a great many interesting people, who are working with us towards the goal of winning the communist world for Christ.

God has called me, in middle age, a semi-invalid who a few years ago was not considered fit even to work behind an office desk, to a most thrilling and satisfying task. The past few years have given me the most rewarding experiences I have ever known.

I attended the first world conference of Missions to the Communist World, where representatives from all the continents had met together to discuss strategy. In an inspiring address, Richard presented us with his vision for the future. He reminded us that our work in the communist countries was only one aspect of a far larger fight.

Ours is a world-wide mission. Our task is to combat communism wherever it is to be found, and wherever it is seeking to gain a foothold — in the universities and labour movements of the West; in the hopes and aspirations of the newly independent countries; in the as yet undeveloped areas of the world.

We must work ceaselessly to help those oppressed by the communists, and at the same time to win the communists and atheists for Christ. We must also awaken our fellow Christians, and those of other religions. We must look not only East, but West, North and South, seeking always and everywhere to turn men's minds away from the false doctrines of the communists to the living truth of the God of the Universe.

There is only one way to do this: by allowing ourselves to be so filled with the Spirit of our Lord and Master in every part of our lives, that we cannot fail to draw many after us. This will be the beginning of a new, bloodless crusade, whose issue can be nothing less than the salvation of the world from the claws of the Red dragon and the preparation of Christ's reign on earth.

The vision is given to a few — to the great ones in God's Kingdom. But the fulfilling of it is the task of the many, the small, the weak, the insignificant, whose duty is simply to get on with the job which lies to hand.

God used me, one of His smallest, to ransom the Wurmbrands. In their turn they, two of His giants, have been used by Him to start a mighty work whose results cannot be calculated this side of Heaven.

The author welcomes correspondence.
Inquiries concerning the underground
church can be sent to

Jesus to the Communist World
P.O. Box 11
Glendale, California 91209